IBRAHIM

*Where in the spectrum
does he belong?*

SHAHIDUN RAHMAN

A young boy's struggle with Semantic Pragmatic Language Disorder

An autobiographical account of a mother's struggle to bring up a child with a learning disorder. It tells the story of Ibrahim Rahman and his struggle with a speech and language disorder, part of the autistic spectrum disorder. It highlights the lack of awareness of this condition within our society, but particularly within the Asian community where autism is not widely recognised.

Edited by Theresa Saliba
www.virtualresources.co.uk

Cover Design by Duncan Bamford
www.insightillustration.co.uk

Paperback: ISBN 1-905399-05-7
13 DIGIT ISBN: 978-1-905399-05-5

Hardback: ISBN 1-905399-00-6
13 DIGIT ISBN: 978-1905399-00-0

REVISED EDITION 2005

Published by
PERFECT PUBLISHERS LTD
23 Maitland Avenue
Cambridge
CB4 1TA
England

ABOUT THE AUTHOR

Shahidun (Shahida) Nessa Rahman was born in Cambridge, England with her twin sister on 14th December 1971, two days before Bangladesh, formerly East Pakistan became independent. She has three older bothers, who were all born and raised in Cambridge and her parents are from Bangladesh.

Ibrahim is the first child of Shahidun and Zillur Rahman. Ibrahim was born in 19th December 1990 in Cambridge. He was a normal, healthy boy and weighed 5lb 15oz. He was an extremely boisterous child who suffered from Semantic Pragmatic Language Disorder, part of the autistic spectrum disorder, and difficulties with his gross motor skills. But it was difficult to explain this to anyone, least of all the family. It affected every aspect of his life. Ibrahim's journey form birth to his teenage years was fraught with problems as he struggled through school. However with grit and determination, he has made excellent progress and is able to live life to the full. His brothers Imran and Aniq experienced delayed speech; but luckily neither of them have developed a language disorder and have since grown in to healthy children.

DEDICATION

This book is dedicated to my twin sister, who is no longer with us today and is missed very much.

I would like to thank my brother Kal, for his help, support and inspiration.

Thank you to Theresa, Duncan and Jan for helping me put this book together.

SEMANTIC PRAGMATIC LANGUAGE DISORDER

Many people hear the term 'autistic' and have some vague idea what it means. Autism is a life-long development disability and effects people in different ways. Autism is a spectrum disorder which means the condition has wide-ranging degrees of severity. You can have a child at one end of the spectrum with barely notice-able traits, whilst another at the other end of the spectrum has full blown autism.

One condition which comes within this spectrum is semantic pragmatic language disorder, a term which has been around for nearly 20 years and was only used to describe children who were not autistic. This was the diagnosis given to my son, Ibrahim, and this book will follow his progress from birth to his teenage years.

Before we commence, it would be useful to look at the common features of SPLD which include:

- delayed language development
- learning to talk by memorising phrases, instead of putting words together freely
- repeating phrases out of context, especially snippets remem-bered from television programmes
- muddling up 'I' and 'you'
- problems with understanding questions, particularly ques-tions involving 'how' and 'why'
- difficulty following conversations

Children with this disorder have difficulty understanding what other people say to them, and they do not understand how to use speech to make themselves understood. Most of the children diagnosed as having semantic pragmatic disorder also have some mild autistic features. For example, they usually have difficulty understanding social situations and may not know what is expected of them. They may also prefer to stick fairly rigidly to routines and often need to have their day planned out for them. They also lack imaginative play and will tend to copy other people rather than think of their own ideas. This is the pattern followed by Ibrahim from about the age of two.

If we break the condition down into its two components, 'Semantics' and 'Pragmatics' we will have a better understanding of what the condition involves and why it develops.

Semantics is the aspect of language function that relates to understanding the meanings of words, phrases and sentences, and using words appropriately when we speak. Children with semantic difficulties have a very hard time understanding the meaning of words and sentences. They may have difficulty processing words that relate to feelings and emotions such as 'upset' and 'worried', abstract words like 'justice' or 'valour', and words that refer to status, for instance 'essential', 'expert' or 'authority'. They often take slang expressions literally or interpret them oddly and they are unable to understand the concept of sarcasm. They may not be able to identify the key point or topic in a sentence and because of this may suddenly make obscure changes to the subject being discussed, apparently thinking they are on the same subject.

Pragmatics is the area of language function that embraces the use of language in social contexts – knowing what to say, how to say it, and when to say it. Children with pragmatic difficulties have great difficulty using language socially. For example, they often do not understand that we take turns to talk, and they will talk over the top of another person, constantly interrupting at inappropriate times. On other occasions, they respond to what you say with inexplicable silences, or in a voice that is too quiet. When they interrupt, which they do excessively, it is usually to talk irrelevantly or to discuss things which the listener shows no interest in so that they appear rude and inconsiderate. They may look around them during a conversation, giving the impression of complete disinterest in what is being discussed.

Children with SPLD have a language disorder that affects both semantic processing and the pragmatics of language use. Some authorities see SPLD as part of the autism spectrum of disorders while others see it purely as a language disorder. It is difficult to make an individual diagnosis because the symptoms vary immensely. Although the mistakes with words and phrases that you are about to encounter with Ibrahim can appear quite amusing, they can be extremely embarrassing and upsetting to the child. It is therefore important that family, peers, teachers and other adults apply great sensitivity in guiding the young person with SPLD.

For more information about Semantic Pragmatic Language Disorder, please visit www.spldinfo.com

'Parents and carers of children with autism will identify with Shahidun and her difficulties with her family, wider society and the Bangladeshi community... making this book a fascinating read.'

Saleem Akhtar
Development officer
BME communities National Autistic Society

CONTENTS

CHAPTER ONE

THE EARLY YEARS – TAKE NOTHING FOR GRANTED

It is difficult for people to imagine the difficulties I had with my eldest child Ibrahim when he was a young child. They look at him now and find it hard to believe that he has had to overcome immense obstacles to get to where he is today. All they see is a polite, well-adjusted young boy who works hard at school and enjoys all the things other boys of his age enjoy. When I look at him, I am filled with pride and admiration because I know how hard Ibrahim had to fight to keep up with his classmates. It was an uphill struggle, but Ibrahim fought all the way and his supreme effort paid off.

Ibrahim Hamzah Rahman was born on 19th December 1990 at the Rosie Maternity Hospital in Cambridge. He was a normal, healthy boy and weighed 5lb 15oz and, because I was of slight build and Ibrahim was my first child, he was a very small baby. In the early months he was fairly contented and grew into a normal toddler, behaving like any other boy of his age. I did notice that he appeared to be exceptionally active and had a never-ending supply of energy, but there was no indication that anything was wrong.

Everything seemed fine up until the age of two years, when Ibrahim had developed into a healthy toddler. It was around this time that my initial concerns for him began to emerge. He babbled constantly and was not saying any recognisable words. It is human nature to talk to our children from the moment they are born and we naturally assume they will learn to talk automatically. By the age of eighteen months, most children can say simple words like dada and mama, but this wasn't the case with Ibrahim. I noticed that other toddlers in my neighbourhood were starting to chatter and say the odd word, but Ibrahim didn't seem capable of uttering any recognisable words. I didn't think anything of it initially because I had no knowledge of language difficulties. I feel it is important for parents to be aware that speech problems exist and that their children may not necessarily develop language skills in the way they expect them to. If we are prepared and know what to expect, we are in a better position to deal with problems as they arise.

Like most parents, I often look back to when my children were young and wonder if I could have done things differently, or if I was in some way to blame for the problems my children encountered. I would like to relate an incident that occurred when Ibrahim was a baby. I am not sure whether this has any bearing on Ibrahim's particular problems, but I feel it is important to mention it just the same. He was about six months old and I had put him in his high chair while I occupied myself with various chores in the kitchen. Because I had not strapped him in securely, he fell out of the chair and hit his head. Although he was thoroughly checked over by our doctor and declared unharmed, I have often wondered whether this had anything to do with his future problems. I have been told that this incident is not related to Ibrahim's learning difficulties, but it has always been at the back of my mind.

Perhaps it would be useful at this point to give you a little background information about my family. My three brothers and twin sister and I were born in Cambridge and our parents were from Bangladesh. My father came to England in 1957 and was one of the first Bangladeshi people to arrive in Cambridge. He started a restaurant soon after arriving and my mother joined him in 1963. In 1990, I entered into an arranged marriage and in February of that year I travelled to Bangladesh to marry Zillur Rahman. I stayed in Bangladesh until July when I returned to Cambridge to fill in the necessary documentation so that Ibrahim's father could join me in England. By this time I was expecting Ibrahim and he was born in December of that year. However, Ibrahim's father wasn't able to join me until he was granted a visa in October 1991, so Ibrahim was ten months old by the time his father saw him. It was a difficult time for all of us and I felt under tremendous pressure trying to adjust to these new circumstances.

When Ibrahim's father first came to this country, he did not know any English, although he has now learned the language. By the time Ibrahim was diagnosed with having difficulties, I found it difficult to make his father understand that Ibrahim had a problem. Ibrahim used to repeat phrases that he had heard somewhere and, because he was saying things in English, his father thought that he was speaking English properly. We were more concerned that he was not able to speak our home language, Bengali, and he felt that this was the initial problem. It was difficult to convince him that Ibrahim was not speaking English correctly, but because he lacked an adequate knowledge of the English language, he was not able to understand this. I had the responsibility of taking Ibrahim to various development checks, and I would try to relay any important information back to his father. I was mentally exhausted as I tried to interpret certain things that were stated in Ibrahim's report so that his father could understand, and this left us both feeling frustrated.

I think we may have expected too much of Ibrahim in the early years. After all, we all thought that he would grow into a normal boy, and his father refused to accept that there was a problem because he looked normal. It was only a few years later that he really began to understand his condition. During Ibrahim's early years, I was left to contend with the difficulties alone and I lacked the advice and support that I so desperately needed. It was difficult coping with Ibrahim's language problem while at the same time trying to make his father understand what I myself was trying to understand. We had never come across something like this before. We all assume that Ibrahim has overcome all his problems and forget the difficulties we still face every day. I understand that Ibrahim's father is the breadwinner and therefore the children spend more time with me and so I understand them more. As for Ibrahim, I feel I know him inside out. I can tell what his facial expressions mean and I know when he is worried, tired or moody.

Ibrahim's father works long hours and the only chance he gets to see the children is after school until about 5.30pm and also on his day off. He does not see them in the morning before he goes to work as they are already at school. His time with them is very limited and, ever since Ibrahim was very young, I have borne most of the child-rearing responsibilities. This is the way the situation has always been and I realised early on that I needed to make the best of it.

I did not experience any language barriers when I was young. My siblings and I spoke Bengali at home and were taught English at school. We never experienced any difficulties using both languages concurrently and I assumed it would be the same with Ibrahim. Everyone spoke Bengali to him as I thought it was important for him to learn this language first. However, he was also exposed to English as this was the language we spoke amongst ourselves. I have since been told that children can take longer to learn to speak if two languages are spoken to them simultaneously. Apparently, processing two languages at the same time requires more determination and effort. Had I known this sooner, I may have been able to prepare myself to deal with Ibrahim's problems more effectively. Should we have spoken just one language at home? Would this have helped Ibrahim's language development? It is difficult to say with certainty whether anything would have made a difference to Ibrahim. After all, how can you prepare yourself for something you do not completely understand?

I remember how concerned I was by Ibrahim's delayed speech, only to be reassured by everyone that he would soon be talking. It was easy to believe this and put the blame for his language problems on the fact that we spoke two languages at home. But I was also concerned about Ibrahim's social behaviour. He was extremely energetic and had stopped taking naps during the day. I wasn't sure whether this was because he didn't need much sleep, or because he was too busy playing to think about rest. Most people assumed that, because of his active schedule and lack of daytime naps, he slept well at night. This was not true – he didn't seem to need any sleep at all! There were not enough hours in the day for him and he didn't want the day to end. He would finally go to sleep well after midnight, only to wake between six and seven o'clock the next morning. I couldn't keep up with him and gradually I began to feel run down and lethargic.

When Ibrahim was two and a half years old we moved into our first home, a two-bedroom maisonette. Up until this time we had lived with my family and Ibrahim was completely spoilt by everyone, particularly by my twin sister who adored him. My sister was a great help to me and, because she knew him better than anyone else, and at times she was able to give me some much needed breathing space. Sometimes she would prepare his meals or give him a bath and put him to bed. Ibrahim grew accustomed to the busy atmosphere at home and loved to be the centre of attention. When we moved to our new home, he became a little subdued and wasn't fully aware of what was happening. I thought the change of scene would be good for him and I hoped the calmer surroundings would make him less energetic.

Very soon after we moved we subscribed to cable television, unaware of the difficulties this would cause. Ibrahim quickly became familiar with the two remote controls, one for the television and one for the cable box. During the time I spent doing the chores, I allowed Ibrahim to watch television. I think all parents like their children to be kept amused when they want to get on with the housework. He got bored quickly with toys, but loved the Cartoon Network channel and I was happy for him to watch it. He watched cartoons for hours and hours and became obsessed with them, learning different phrases and parroting them at home. We also had teletext and Ibrahim soon learnt how to use this too. He was clever enough to check the television listings and we eventually had to put a parental control on the cartoon channel to reduce his hours in front of the television. Unfortunately, this was not enough to stop Ibrahim's obsession. He was so fascinated with numbers that he was able to work out the pin number to get the restriction removed and we had to change it at least four times. He spent hours trying to discover how things worked and even learnt to use the calculator settings on the remote control.

Because of his obsession with television controls, it was difficult to persuade Ibrahim to change channels, especially in front of guests. They probably thought he was such a disobedient boy who refused to listen to his mother. When we asked him if we could watch a different channel, he would become rebellious and throw a tantrum, screaming and shouting and refusing to cooperate. He became angry if he didn't get his own way and there was no compromising. I usually found it easier to give in to him; it was the only way of getting peace, although I knew it wasn't the right thing to do.

Ibrahim's father was firmer than I was. He did not fully understand Ibrahim's speech difficulties and he thought that teaching him Bengali would solve all his problems. As I have already explained, because he could hear that Ibrahim was able to speak English, I was constantly trying to convince him that he really did have a serious speech and language difficulty. At the same time, I was trying to deal with Ibrahim's problems myself and the strain was increasing every day.

We eventually returned the cable television after much consideration, deciding it would be better for Ibrahim. He wasn't able to accept us telling him, "You can't watch television until after breakfast." He just couldn't understand what it meant, so he refused to listen. Whenever Ibrahim wasn't able to understand what he was being told, he would stop paying attention and start to ignore me completely. I think he felt that, if he pretended I wasn't there, I would go away and he could do as he wished.

All of Ibrahim's awkward behavioural problems were connected to his speech problem, although I didn't realise this at the time. I thought that he was deliberately being disobedient; although I was aware that he was not able to understand many of the things he was told. My life and experience of dealing with Ibrahim at that time was a combination of anger, frustration and confusion. Was he truly being naughty or did he really have behavioural difficulties? I asked myself this question so many times and the same thoughts were forever going around my head, making it difficult for me to switch off and relax. I remember wishing it was all a dream, which I still do sometimes. It is my way of coping.

If Ibrahim needed something, he would pull me by the hand to the object that he wanted and point to it. Most of the time it was difficult to understand him, so I decided the best thing to do was to learn Ibrahim's language. It was vital for me to comprehend what he was trying to say to me and, surprisingly, it was not as difficult as I thought. Most mothers can understand the language their children use, even when no one else does. I thought that finally I would be able to break through the communication barrier that existed between Ibrahim and those around him. However, things were not going to be that simple.

CHAPTER 2

THE HIDDEN DISORDER

Ibrahim started Brunswick Nursery School in September 1994. He had an afternoon place from 1 pm until 3.30 pm and I was thrilled on his first day. I believed that being surrounded by other children would help develop Ibrahim's language and also help him overcome his difficulties. At that time I didn't realise how serious his language difficulties were and I didn't fully understand his problems. As it turned out, he didn't spend much time with the children outside school hours, but instead he spent most of his time at home, growing up with adults around him. In hindsight, I really don't think it would have made any difference if he had grown up with other children. I began to realise that language was something he had to learn in his own way, even if it was going to take a long time.

Ibrahim had only just stopped wearing nappies and, much to my relief, he was toilet trained by the time he started nursery school. By the age of four, he had learnt the English alphabet by heart. Ibrahim never went through the stage of learning the alphabet as 'a-ber-cer', the way his schoolmates did. He learnt to read the letters as 'a-b-c' and he could also read a few words. I was unsure about whether he was remembering words rather than reading them, but I was happy that his reading and number counting skills were advanced for his age. He could count up to 100 and could count backwards too, and if we chose a number at random, he would be able to read it without hesitation. He was mesmerised by numbers, especially big ones such as three-figure numbers. I was convinced he had a photo-graphic memory because he was able to visualise things in his head and remember them well. I believe his photographic memory has played a vital part in enabling him to process language. Before long, Ibrahim was reading numbers into the thousands. Because he was the only child in his nursery school who knew the alphabet off by heart and numbers up to 100, it was easy to assume that there was nothing wrong with him.

Ibrahim was slowly learning new words and trying to put them into sentences, but most of what he said made little sense. People were often confused to hear Ibrahim talking nonsense. After all, in their minds he was a healthy young boy who was advanced in number and letter reading, yet he spoke gibberish. I heard the same comment a hundred times when people would say, 'He looks all right to me!' Most people believe that a disability has to be seen physically in order for it to be real and fully understood. After all, how can one understand something they cannot see? I often wondered whether a language difficulty could be classed as a type of disability. I know that a speech impediment is regarded as a type of disability, but perhaps the word 'disability' is too strong a word to be used regarding speech and language difficulties. With Ibrahim, you couldn't see that there was anything wrong with him. It was as if his knowledge of language was 'disabled' in some way, rather than Ibrahim himself being disabled. That is the way I believe it should be viewed.

It was around this time that Ibrahim first learnt to use a computer, which he enjoyed immensely. Computers were the number one thing in his life – they were his best friends and he related to them better than he could relate to people. Computers did what he wanted them to do and they listened to him without expecting anything in return. Press a button and hey presto, there you have it! Sometimes I almost believed that he wished I was as easy to control as a computer. The keyboard fascinated him and it didn't take him long to work out how to turn the computer on and off, and he quickly grasped the purpose of computer programs.

There were even times at his nursery school when the teachers asked Ibrahim for assistance with their computers. It was amazing how Ibrahim was able to focus so well on computer work, but not as well on other tasks.

Ibrahim's memory at this young age never ceased to amaze me. When I took him out in his pushchair, I told him the names of the different cars as we passed them. It didn't take him long before he was able to name certain makes of car, such as Peugeot and Ford. He knew most of the names of the roads we took and it was even possible to leave him in the middle of the street a short distance from home, and Ibrahim would be able to find his way back.

Ibrahim started to wear glasses in September 1994 after an eye test proved he was short-sighted. He needed to wear them all the time, but typically he didn't like them at first. It took him quite a while to get used to them, but he eventually did. I was disappointed that he needed to wear glasses permanently. In my extended family, I couldn't think of any child who had needed to wear glasses at such a young age, but then I couldn't think of a child who had suffered from language difficulties either – someone had to be first and it was Ibrahim.

When he attended nursery, I worked at the Cambridge Citizens' Advice Bureau as a volunteer. I had previously trained for six months' prior to Ibrahim starting school when I sent him to a day nursery once a week. He had trouble settling in and it was difficult to leave him. He screamed and clung to me as if he thought he would never see me again. His young mind just couldn't understand why I wanted to leave him there. I was virtually in tears when I walked out of the nursery, and felt as if I was being incredibly cruel to him. Ibrahim had lunch there but did not eat a thing, although the nursery assistants tried very hard to encourage him. I even considered leaving the training course because of Ibrahim until my mother decided that she would look after him while I trained. This solved my problems as I knew he would enjoy spending time with his nana and I would not need to worry about him any more. Just as I completed the training, my mother fell ill.

She was diagnosed with angina and had to spend a week in hospital. Ibrahim and I spent most days there and he would happily snuggle up next to my mother in her bed. He liked it there and was very understanding about his nana being ill.

In time I was required to work two afternoons a week from 1 p.m. until 4.30 p.m. It seemed a very long time and invariably I ended up worrying about Ibrahim. His father had to take care of him because I could not leave him with his nana now due to her health problems. When it came to mealtimes, I knew his father would not be as persistent with Ibrahim as I was. He would ask him if he wanted something to eat, and if Ibrahim said no, he wouldn't try to coax him any further. I knew that Ibrahim needed encouragement to eat and he had to be asked repeatedly or he would go without food for hours. During school hours, I was only required to work 1.15 p.m. until 3.15 p.m. five days a week. The school was just five minutes away from the bureau which was very convenient for me and I knew that Ibrahim was very happy there so I didn't need to worry about him. School was the best place for him and it was a huge relief that he had settled in well.

I enjoyed my work as it taught me to be patient and calm in difficult situations with clients. I was trained to listen to people, which was something I knew I needed to improve on. It taught me valuable lessons which I would always remember and it affected the way I related to others, especially Ibrahim. I became more sympathetic and understanding and eventually moved on to an employed post at the bureau. Even though I was only there for a few hours a week, I really enjoyed my time at the bureau. It was a chance to get away from the stress of having to cope with Ibrahim's language difficulties and demanding behaviour.

I used to take Ibrahim to work with me during the school holidays, and he was quite happy to sit in the corner of the room and play with the toys. I remember one time when we were alone in one of the rooms, Ibrahim decided to press the panic button (this was only pressed if there was a problem with a client and the situation was becoming difficult). Everyone rushed downstairs from the main office and I didn't realise what he had done until two of the senior staff entered the room. I was extremely embarrassed and explained what had happened, but Ibrahim didn't understand the seriousness of his actions. Luckily, my colleagues found the whole thing hilarious and talked about it for days afterwards.

During his nursery year, an educational psychologist assessed Ibrahim and diagnosed him as having specific language difficulties. This was the first step in a long history of assessments. Although he was able to talk, he was unable to make sense of using language correctly and was unable to express himself clearly. His vocabulary was limited for his age and was the level of a two year old. After his assessment a report was written and this was used for his referral to primary school. I was relieved that something concrete was being done about Ibrahim's problems, and in a way I felt vindicated. At last other people were acknowledging what I had known for so long – that Ibrahim had a communication problem and needed help.

Despite the daily problems faced by Ibrahim, he enjoyed nursery school so much that he didn't want to go home at the end of the school day. There were times when we would be the last ones out of the school due to his persistence in playing on the slide in the playground. It was a way of keeping Ibrahim happy so that I could take him home without any fuss, but we always ended up having to hurry as we had a bus to catch. At times it was a nightmare collecting Ibrahim from school. Although I looked forward to seeing him and would rush from work to collect him, he didn't want to go home. When the teacher opened the classroom door for all the parents to come in and collect their children, Ibrahim would pretend he hadn't seen me and would carry on playing or pretending to read a book. I literally had to stare him in the face to get his attention. Sometimes he would hit me and knock my glasses off my face, which was awful and humiliating and I wanted the earth to swallow me up. I didn't know how to handle the situation and was always concerned about what the other parents would think.

It may seem hard for others to believe, but I had to drag him out of school on many occasions, crying, screaming, kicking and yelling, 'I don't want to go home now!' He loved school so much and would happily have spent all his time there. Other parents stared disapprovingly as I struggled to control Ibrahim, desperately trying to drag him from the classroom. They took their children out of school without any fuss and I often looked on enviously as the other children walked happily home. Why couldn't it be like that for me? I thought it was a phase Ibrahim was going through and hoped it would pass, and I was right because eventually it did. After weeks of assistance from the teachers, Ibrahim started to accept home time and at last I started to enjoy taking him to school.

We always took a bus to and from school which meant that Ibrahim had to have lunch early at home, although he never ate much. At the bus stop we met all sorts of people and I recognised a few regulars who caught the same bus each day. Ibrahim had echolalia which meant that he constantly repeated phrases he had heard. These phrases were mainly from television programmes, especially game shows which fascinated him. He would repeat the same thing over and over again, for example, 'You now have ten points!' People found this amusing but I found it embarrassing. He knew exactly which bus we had to take to different places and he also knew when to press the 'bus stopping' button when it was nearly time for us to get off. I was always in a rush because if we missed our bus, we had to wait for at least half an hour for the next one and Ibrahim wasn't a patient boy. On the journey home we talked about many things, but mainly we discussed what Ibrahim had done at school that day. It was a valuable time for both of us when we could sit down together and talk about many things. He was usually very fidgety and found it difficult to sit still, and this is something that he still has a problem with today.

Even when he was ill, Ibrahim hated being off school. He would complain bitterly about wanting to go as he didn't really understand that he had to be kept away from school to get better. School gave him a routine; it gave him a chance to play with other children and, of course, learn new things. He needed a routine to follow everyday because without it he was completely lost. It was difficult at holiday times when Ibrahim would wonder why he was away from school for so long. He did not understand about dates or holidays or how long they would last, and he had no real concept of time. Ibrahim lived in the 'now' and he could not comprehend 'tomorrow' or 'next week'. This lack of understanding added to his impatience and was totally frustrating for me to deal with.

It was a sad time when Ibrahim finished nursery. He hadn't particularly made any friends, but by the end of the nursery year, Ibrahim knew the names of every child in his class and played alongside them. Playing with children and playing alongside them are two different things. He wasn't able to interact with other children in the correct manner; his poor social skills were to blame. He was aggressive during play and would tug and pull at the other children because this was his way of communicating. The children didn't understand that Ibrahim had learning difficulties and he didn't realise the wrong he was doing and therefore many children avoided him.

At this time, Ibrahim's verbal comprehension was assessed as being equal to a child aged two years and eight months. This assessment compared his ability at naming vocabulary to others in his age group. He would pronounce a chair as 'a chairs', a box as 'a boxes', a cup was 'a cup of tea' and a spade was 'sand and bucket'. When he was unable to name an object, he attempted to use language he knew to identify it rather than admit he didn't know. Ibrahim always compelled himself to give an answer whether or not it was relevant to the subject, and he was very quick in doing so.

I had to speak to him in English as it was the only way we were able to communicate with each other, but he understood very little because his expressive and receptive language skills were delayed for his age. He spoke no Bengali at all which made it difficult when we were around family because we spoke Bengali to each other. People assumed that Ibrahim spoke fluent Bengali and were shocked when I told them he couldn't speak it. They used to try to talk to him in Bengali, but he never said anything in reply and they blamed me for teaching him to speak English first and not our mother tongue. Even his father suggested that I was at fault, which to me felt like a slap in the face. They had to blame someone and of course it had to be me because mothers are always blamed for their children's failings. I was made to feel useless and a failure and I hated to think that Ibrahim would be labelled. However, I have now learned to accept the way Ibrahim is and I don't worry about the opinion of others as much as I used to. It has taken a great deal of time and patience to reach this stage in my life and it was difficult road to travel, but it has been worth it.

As if I didn't have enough to cope with, sleeping through the night without disturbance was also a problem. Ibrahim's bed was positioned beside ours. Although he slept near me, he felt insecure at night and didn't like sleeping in his bed near the wall and he would wake up constantly. To get a decent nights' sleep I allowed Ibrahim to sleep in our bed, which I very soon realised was a bad mistake. He grew so used to sleeping with us that we couldn't persuade him to sleep in his own bed. At times, when he fell asleep in my arms, I would put him in his bed, but he would wake up in the middle of the night and get back into our bed. I didn't make a fuss at the time because I was so exhausted and desperately needed my sleep. We decided that we had to make him sleep in his own bed because he was so fidgety at night that we were all having trouble sleeping. Ibrahim cried bitterly about this for a few long nights, but I was determined that he would not get his own way this time. Eventually he did sleep in his own bed without any fuss, but I still kept his bed in our room. Some people may find this strange because most children sleep alone in their own rooms from a very young age, but I felt Ibrahim was not ready for this stage. He had always been clingy and I had to wait until the time was right before I made any drastic changes to his routine.

Ibrahim's appetite was deteriorating day after day. He preferred to snack and was starting to be fussy about the foods he ate. At school he refused to eat any food or drink offered to him at snack time. He disliked fruit and vegetables and he wasn't keen on meat, chicken or fish even though he had eaten these foods when he was a baby. I was constantly concerned about his diet and my nagging wasn't helping either me or Ibrahim. I had tried almost everything, but it was no good. I always felt that I was doing something wrong and it was very tempting to give up and admit defeat.

Ibrahim also had problems with his fine and gross motor skills which were below average for his age. He was able to ride a bicycle with stabilizers but he did fall off quite a bit as his legs were weak and lacked strength. A simple task such as pouring himself a drink also presented him with difficulties and he wasn't able to pour it without spilling most of it. He also found it difficult to feed himself and, although he did try, he was very slow and messy and I found it easier to feed him myself. It was heartbreaking and frustrating to watch him make such a supreme effort yet still be left struggling with the most basic life skills.

It was a worrying time for me when the time came for Ibrahim to move on to full-time school. In August 1995, during the summer holidays, Ibrahim was asked to attend thirteen separate hour-long speech therapy sessions with other children who had similar difficulties. The therapist stated that he showed some improvement in active participation but he still found it difficult to take turns. His performance varied depending on how well focused he was. It was typical of Ibrahim to echo the responses of others to feel part of the group and he tended to repeat language he had heard previously, even though it was irrelevant to the situation. However, he enjoyed going to these groups very much and benefited from the sessions. Now, as he took the important step to full-time school, I wondered how he would cope.

CHAPTER 3

EXPECT THE UNEXPECTED

In September 1995, Ibrahim started his reception year at Arbury Primary School which had a separate speech and language unit for children with specific language disorders. The school was very near home, but I was concerned about whether he could cope with the long hours. The first few days were difficult for him and he was tearful in the beginning, but he coped better than I expected. He was particularly interested in number books and I was happy to encourage this interest. When he went to his classroom in the morning he was expected to choose a reading book and sit on the carpet to read it. Typically, most days Ibrahim would choose the same book. He also had problems paying attention and looked around in class without contributing; his mind just seemed to be elsewhere.

After a few weeks, he was able to name all the children in his class in the order they were listed on the register. His teacher reported that he was alert if she asked 'Who will take the register?' and he even remembered whose turn it was to take the register to the school office. He still found it hard to play or interact with the other children; he continued to play alongside them, but did not really join in conversations. He didn't greet the children or teachers and teaching him to say hello when he met people took some time. Ibrahim was able to complete jigsaws very quickly compared to his classmates because he was able to put them together by memory by visualising the pictures in his head. He was also very interested in

Lego bricks and any other toys that involved constructing things and sometimes he would spend hours playing with them, completely losing track of time.

Ibrahim's play was rather stereotyped and repetitive. Most of the time he enjoyed playing alone with his imaginary friends which is something many children do. He played in a solitary way and chatted constantly as if there was someone else playing with him. He tended to isolate himself from the outside world as if there was an invisible barrier surrounding him. When I called him he wouldn't listen and I had to call him a number of times to catch his attention. He exhibited the same behaviour at school and I often wondered whether he could hear me or whether he simply chose not to. At times I knew he was deliberately ignoring me; Ibrahim only wanted to listen when it suited him, otherwise he was quite happy to continue playing in his own little world.

Ibrahim imitated the good and bad behaviour of other children, not knowing what was right or wrong. He didn't listen to what the other children were saying to him and some children didn't like Ibrahim getting too close. He was unable to read the signals they gave him and didn't understand peoples' feelings and so he was unable to respond to them. He talked at children rather than with them and he made irrelevant comments which baffled those around him. Children found his behaviour strange because they were too young to realise he had communication problems. I think most people who knew Ibrahim labelled him as being strange, which is a difficult thing for a parent to accept. In role-play situations he imitated things he had seen adults doing because he lacked imagination. Although he was able to accurately mimic others, he was unable to develop his own ideas. Ibrahim didn't really establish friendly relationships with the teachers and helpers because he didn't show any interest in them or in what they were doing. He had developed some very bad behaviour traits and would bite people, not realising how painful this was. He did this to me many times and he also hit me during his many tantrums. I realised it was part of his behaviour and something I had to learn to accept until Ibrahim was mature enough to control himself.

Lunch was served in the classroom during the first term so that the children could get used to the routine of school. Ibrahim hardly ate a thing and I had to sit with him at lunch time to encourage him to eat. I expected him to copy the eating habits of his classmates, but he wasn't the slightest bit interested in food. Because I was concerned about his poor eating habits I decided to take him home for lunch, but even then I couldn't persuade him to eat much. When I took him back to school each day, I was invariably feeling angry and frustrated and I continued to worry about his diet. He had developed many bad habits and would only eat small amounts if he had his toys with him or was watching television. Although I knew this was not the best way to deal with the situation, I gave in to Ibrahim's demands because I was desperate to see him eat.

I remember one occasion when I shouted at him all the way to school because he had refused to eat any lunch. As he went into the classroom he saw a friend and sat next to him and told him tearfully, 'My mum went mad!' When I heard this I felt like a complete monster and his words and pitiful expression haunted me all the way home. By the time I reached my front door, all my pent-up emotion was released and I broke down and cried. I was totally obsessed with the idea of getting Ibrahim to eat and this had caused me to become unbalanced so that I began to take all my frustrations out on him. His poor eating was seriously affecting me and all I could think about was ways to improve it. I felt hurt and guilty and desperately needed to know where I was going wrong.

Ibrahim would go without food for hours and not tell me that he was hungry. Food was becoming a big issue because he refused to eat proper meals, so I was constantly fretting about his diet. He disliked most of the food we ate as a family and he didn't like crisps, chocolates or drinks, not even juices or fizzy drinks. To this day he still refuses to eat crisps and he takes this dislike to bizarre extremes and won't even touch a packet. If anyone ate crisps or a particular food he disliked in his presence, he quietly moved away and left the room.

Most children have a sandwich, a packet of crisps and yoghurt in their packed lunches. Ibrahim didn't eat any of these so I used to give him small pieces of cheese and tomato pizza, or chapatti. Although he ate these at home he wouldn't eat them if they were given to him at school and every day his lunch box came back untouched. Some days I gave him cream crackers with cheese, but if they were broken in any way he wouldn't eat them. On one occasion his drink leaked inside his packed lunch box and made his crackers soggy. Although he hardly ever ate his lunch, he complained that if his drink hadn't leaked he would have eaten it this time. I think it was important for him to bring it back home dry; that was what concerned him, not the fact that he couldn't eat it.

Ibrahim was able to name foods that he liked by the end of the reception year. For example, he liked 'Linda McCartney's deep country pies' and I gave him one every day because this was the only food he would eat. He still went for hours without eating as if he had to be reminded to eat. Eventually I realised I had to accept that Ibrahim had difficulties eating as well as difficulties with his speech. The pressures were building up and it was difficult for me to accept that Ibrahim would never eat certain foods. I was forced to be exceptionally patient and I constantly reminded myself to stop nagging him. My battles with Ibrahim over his diet were beginning to take over my life completely, and I knew I needed to take a few steps back and give him space.

During Ibrahim's reception year his fine motor skills improved considerably, although there were still some difficulties. He was able to trace over letters and could even form them himself, but he couldn't do this accurately. He found it difficult to use scissors which he found easier to hold with both hands and the only cutting he ever did were straight lines. It took him at least another three years to hold scissors properly and to be able to cut out complex shapes. He couldn't colour in pictures properly and also found painting difficult. His drawings were immature for his age and I knew Ibrahim didn't particularly enjoy these activities which was another reason why he felt he didn't need to make a great effort.

One thing Ibrahim really enjoyed was singing, but he found it hard to clap a simple rhythm; he much preferred playing instruments. I remember Ibrahim's first school play. He was chosen to be a 'surfer' and he had to imagine he was on a beach in Hawaii. There were four other children with him and most of the time he just copied them, imitating their actions. At times Ibrahim would fiddle with his t-shirt and would pull it up and down, not realizing what he was doing. I remember mouthing to him from the audience, 'Pull your t-shirt down!' because I was worried that the other children would laugh at him.

Ibrahim's gross motor skills in comparison to his fine motor skills were poor and below average for his age. This wasn't helped by the fact that he was very thin. His arms were skinny and he bumped into things, which I assumed was because he had little spatial awareness. He was unable to kick or catch a ball properly and working on the PE apparatus at school was a great struggle. Ibrahim would hold out his hands to catch a ball, but found it difficult to reach out in the direction it was coming from. By the time he had worked this out, it was often too late and the ball had already fallen to the ground. Most of the time he felt disappointed with himself because he always tried so hard and his effort seemed wasted.

Ibrahim became nervous if things did not happen the way he expected them to. He became anxious about new situations or changes in routines that he had become familiar with. He didn't favour working independently because he felt lost and he preferred to rely on adult support to steer him in the right direction; this is something he still needs now. Ibrahim was very dependant on fixed rules, but he could only manage one instruction at a time. It had to be made very clear and simple for him to understand and his dependence on detailed routine was to an unusual degree. For example; his classroom displayed a calendar and a weather chart and they were usually changed most days. There were times they were left unchanged, for instance on a Monday morning they would still be displaying Friday's information. Ibrahim would head straight for the calendar and weather chart to correct them before he would do anything else. He would talk about the calendar as if it was a very important part of the school day; it had to be just right.

Ibrahim was very motivated by rewards such as stickers, which had 'Well done!' written on them, but they only worked on a short-term basis. He loved them and tried to gain them almost everyday and looked forward to receiving 'smilies' – little 'smiley faces' stamped on the back of the hand as a reward. He preferred the red ones to the green ones and this mattered to him so much that at the end of the day Ibrahim refused to have them washed off.

Ibrahim was put on the outreach programme at the Arbury Speech and Language Centre, which was based at the school he was attending. He received five hours a week support from central funds in recognition of his problems. It was good that he was getting some support but I felt five hours was not enough because he needed intensive help for longer hours. I knew he would benefit if they increased the hours but I was grateful for any help that was forthcoming.

At the time he wasn't considered to have a speech impediment, stammer or block before initiating speech. He was unusually quiet in the classroom and his teacher thought this was due to a lack of understanding in what was happening. Ibrahim had a poor comprehension of the events around him such as reading, listening and visually interpreting pictures. These were all language skills that needed to be learnt, but if it all became too much, he would switch off. He never talked about 'when I was small' or 'where I live' and was confused by such concepts. Generally, life was too difficult for him to make sense of and every day was a struggle.

Although his behaviour was generally good at school and at home, his obsessions about certain aspects of the school day had a detrimental effect on his learning. The calendar and the computer both seemed to dominate his day at school, affecting his behaviour and work. If the computer was on at school, it totally absorbed his concentration. Even when he went to his nana's house, the Nintendo dominated his time there. It became more important to him than anything else.

When we went shopping, I usually avoided going to the shops that had small cars and trains for children to ride on because Ibrahim was always very persistent about having a ride. One go was not enough for him and he always wanted to carry on riding, refusing to get off. He would scream loudly, not understanding that it was time to go. I had to force him off and into his pushchair, which didn't look good and passers-by probably thought that I was being cruel. After that, I always avoided taking him anywhere near rides like these. There were so many situations I had to avoid because of Ibrahim's difficult behaviour but I was determined he would not always get what he wanted.

Ibrahim's uncle got married in September 1995, which meant travelling to Brighton for the wedding. I didn't feel comfortable about going because I was unsure how Ibrahim would react and I considered not going. However, it was the first wedding of all my brothers and I didn't want to miss it so I felt compelled to go. I knew that, as we would be absent from home, Ibrahim would eat very little or absolutely nothing. I was also worried that he would not sit quietly as it was difficult to control him and I expected him to misbehave. At the wedding he met a few children of his own age and some that were older. There was an elevator at the centre where the reception took place and Ibrahim was instantly attracted to it. He spent hours going up and down in it and it was surprising it didn't break down. I pulled him away from it many times and told him firmly to stop using it because he was being a nuisance. He didn't listen, not because he wanted to be disobedient, but because he didn't understand that he was doing anything wrong. He spent the day constantly giggling, laughing and getting over-excited. Nothing else mattered to him apart from the elevator and he just carried on happily until it was time to go home.

As I expected, he didn't eat a thing, which was not surprising as he was too busy playing. Ibrahim didn't even drink a sip of water. I was surprised he was not thirsty, what with all the running around he did. This was Ibrahim's first outing away from Cambridge. We never took him away from home on long journeys because his behaviour always prevented us from doing so. There was the added problem that he wouldn't eat anything away from home and we missed out on doing many things with him because of this. Although I found this restrictive, I knew it was not his fault.

Most parents enjoy taking their children out for a meal, to McDonalds perhaps. They go shopping, visit the cinema or do other activities with them. The only place I took Ibrahim was to the park where he would run around freely. I avoided taking him shopping, because he was difficult and demanded to buy many things. It was hard to compromise with him and he would just make a scene and people would stare. It was difficult not to let other peoples' reactions bother me. Even a trip to the park proved frustrating because he never wanted to go home and we always came back with him upset and tearful. It was a strain trying to keep him happy, yet this was what I was trying to do all the time.

Ibrahim did enjoy going to his nana's house. It was like his second home and he felt at ease there. My sister and brothers took care of him, although they too found him difficult. He was close to my sister who understood him and was very patient. She was more tolerant with him than anyone else in the family, including myself. She enjoyed taking him out and spoilt him with gifts, especially at birthdays and Eid celebrations. He was the only nephew in the family and he turned to her if he needed to express anything. They had a very close and loving relationship and I knew that Ibrahim loved her dearly.

From the age of two, Ibrahim was crazy about Nintendo and play stations. He was fascinated by these games and would sit down with his uncles and play happily until he learnt how to do so independently. He was able to reach levels that other children his age were not able to achieve. He played Nintendo games every time he visited his nana's house as it was the only way of keeping him quiet and happy. At times he played for hours and the hardest part was getting him to stop playing. It became a battle of wills and it was very easy to give in to him sometimes, if not all of the time. Giving him the things he wanted was the only way of keeping him happy. My mother would rather have him sitting quietly than running around all over the house. She liked a quiet environment and I was conscious of keeping him occupied and quiet when I visited her. Although it seemed as though I used his speech and behavioural difficulties as an excuse for him, it was not an excuse. It was the way Ibrahim was and it was something that he had little control over.

On one occasion, my brothers and their families came to visit my mother's house when we were visiting too. To keep Ibrahim occupied, we let him play on the Nintendo. As he had been playing a long time I told him it was time to switch it off. He threw a tantrum, angrily kicking and screaming, and he even bit a hole in my dress. My family watched and must have thought, 'What a naughty boy, why doesn't he listen to his mother?' I was so embarrassed. Their looks said it all and I just didn't know what to say or do, so I froze. Situations like this wore me down and I used to say to myself, 'Why can't he be normal?' I became more and more anxious, knowing that a situation like this could easily arise whenever Ibrahim was challenged. I had to teach myself to stay calm and deal with the situation in a more controlled manner. I still have the dress today and when I look at the hole, it strongly reminds me of Ibrahim's difficulties. I've told Ibrahim about this incident and he finds it difficult to believe that he could have done something as bad as this.

By the end of the reception year, Ibrahim was able to sit quietly and listen to stories read to him. He was gradually improving in many ways but there was still a long way to go. Ibrahim had a cousin who was four months older and he was often compared to him, although not intentionally. It seemed like a competition and I was losing all the time. I felt inferior because some people, especially from my community, were ignorant of Ibrahim's problems. They purely judged him on his behaviour and did not try to find out why he may be acting in this way. I wasn't able to understand the situation fully myself, so how could I expect anyone else to? I had no knowledge of speech and language difficulties until Ibrahim was diagnosed with this condition.

We have a large family and I often wondered whether Ibrahim's difficulties could have been inherited. However, as I have already mentioned, I don't know of anyone in the family diagnosed with the same problems as Ibrahim. His father had a problem with stuttering when he was younger but he had simply grown out of it, but I sometimes felt it might have something to do with that. Because he has an above average knowledge of words and numbers, over the years I have had to convince people that Ibrahim really does have a speech and language disorder. Even when I took the time to explain his condition to others, most simply said, 'He looks normal to me' or 'He can speak well'. Many people think that if you have a language problem, this means you would be unable to speak at all. It is also true that people only respond to some form of physical disability, and if it isn't visible, it doesn't exist. It's like judging a book by its cover and not knowing what's inside. Ibrahim was like a book and one has to really get to know him to understand him.

Most Bangladeshi parents naturally expect their children to learn Bengali as their first language. Children learn the language at home through their parents and I wanted this for Ibrahim because it was our mother tongue. When he went to nursery he learnt English gradually, but he learnt Bengali much later. One of his difficulties was in processing language and Bengali was harder for him to learn. Today he is able to speak fluent Bengali. The language structure is different and the word order is different to that of English. For example, 'I'm going to have a bath' would be said as, 'I'm bath going to have.' This language structure fuels the difficulties more and it is confusing for him to try to make sense of English and Bengali too.

Initially, I tried my best to explain Ibrahim's problems to other people, but it seemed to them that I was making excuses for his behaviour. After a while it was easier not to bother at all. I had been too concerned by what other people thought about Ibrahim, but as I began to understand his problems, it did not matter any more. I realised that I should be grateful for the good qualities he possessed and I was proud of his many talents. I have since learned to keep conversations short and sweet with people who do not know us very well. I am tired of explaining over and over again and going round in circles. I know now that it is important to accept a situation if you want to move on to better things.

Many people wanted to pinpoint a reason for Ibrahim's hyperactive behaviour and some blamed it on his obsession with Nintendo games. I was also told that I wasn't teaching him to eat the right foods, that I wasn't firm enough with him and that I let him get away with too much. I listened to many opinions, especially from my mother. I felt guilty, as though everything was my fault because I should have done more to help develop his language when he was much younger. People can either be encouraging or discouraging with their comments. The majority of people who had firm opinions on Ibrahim's behaviour problems had no knowledge of his condition. They simply voiced their views, blamed me for his difficulties, and didn't stop to think how hurtful their remarks were. Through this, I have learnt not to be too quick to judge others and always listen to the facts first.

Ibrahim worked closely with an outreach teacher from the Arbury Speech and Language Centre who assessed him in different skills. One day, his teacher went to collect Ibrahim from his classroom where he was working. She approached him and asked him if he would like to work with her. He replied, 'No,' but got up and followed her. She told him that she had left something in the car, to which he replied, 'We'd better go and get it then.' She looked at Ibrahim and asked, 'Are you coming with me?' Ibrahim replied, 'No'. This is a simple example of Ibrahim's inability to understand the current situation. His responses do not align with his actions. Another time he said, 'Is it raining outside?' 'Yes it's raining and it's very cold,' his teacher replied. Ibrahim thought for a moment and said, 'Yes, but, where's the fire?' The expression he used was appropriate, but he had not acknowledged the context or the association he had made between the rain and the cold. Ibrahim was shown a picture of a child covered in paint and was asked why he was dirty. He responded, 'He's got all over on him'. This is just a typical example of the difficulties Ibrahim had in using language. Although he had a good idea of what he wanted to say, he had problems putting sentences together and was unable to convey his own understanding. He was frustrated, because he was not able to express himself the way that he wanted to.

Ibrahim started year one in September 1996. He still needed help in developing his listening skills, social skills, and his fine and gross motor skills, but most important of all he needed help in all areas of the curriculum, especially literacy and numeracy. The truth was he needed help in all aspects of his life. Ibrahim went to the Arbury Speech and Language Centre for one session a week, usually on a Thursday morning from September 1996 until January 1997. Surprisingly, he felt very much at home there and he was comfortable in a small group of no more than ten children. Ibrahim instantly made friends, whereas he had not found it easy in a large class. I used to collect him for dinner and it was not easy to take him away, even for just half an hour. He felt comfortable there and did not want to go home because he was very happy.

By this time his statement of educational needs was being monitored closely. I had to write a report for the education authority in July 1996 and this was the first step in receiving the much needed specialist help. At first I could not even think what to write as it was difficult to put the details down on paper. It took a great deal of thinking because I did not fully understand the difficulties Ibrahim had to cope with. His educational psychologist, who was an independent doctor and specialised in speech difficulties, and Ibrahim's speech therapist also submitted reports. It was decided that Ibrahim should be placed in the speech and language centre at his mainstream school full time. I was delighted by this decision, as now he would be able to get specialist help and hopefully progress with his difficulties. At first I found it confusing trying to understand the statement of educational needs because it was all new to me. However, the information I was given helped me and the people involved were extremely sympathetic and understanding.

When Ibrahim was in year one, his teacher requested that parents' help with reading groups in the morning from 9 a.m.–9 30 a.m. This meant sitting with a group of children who would read to the parent. I immediately volunteered, viewing it as an opportunity to see Ibrahim and be involved with his class. Ibrahim was not in the group I was helping and he would wave to me happily as soon as he saw me enter the classroom. However, during the reading sessions, his attitude seemed to change. He wouldn't look at me directly and I sensed that he was jealous and angry and when my eyes met his, he would give me an angry look. At first I wondered why he was like this, as I had not done anything to aggravate him. I began to think that perhaps he did not want to see me at school during his lessons. That first evening, I was desperate to know what was causing him difficulties and I asked him why he had acted strangely as it had been playing on my mind all afternoon. Ibrahim explained that he wanted me to help in his reading group and he thought that it was unfair that I was not helping him, but helping other children in another reading group. I told him that I was placed in that group because the previous helper had left and that he already had a helper in his group. Although I knew it wouldn't be easy, I decided that I would continue to give half an hour twice a week. Ibrahim had to realise that he could not always have what he wanted and that life did not revolve around him one hundred per cent.

Unfortunately, his jealousy continued for a few weeks and it was difficult to deal with. I explained the same thing after every session, but it was not getting through to him, which angered me more. I even told his teacher to have a word with him, hoping this would help the situation. I eventually had to give up these sessions, not because of Ibrahim, but because of other commitments. In a way, it was a relief for me. However I did feel angry that Ibrahim had put me through this.

CHAPTER 4

DIAGNOSIS AND TREATMENT

In January 1997, Ibrahim transferred to the Arbury Speech and Language centre. He already knew all the children and staff there, so he didn't have any trouble in settling down. Ibrahim was excited about this and he was always made to feel welcome. This put my mind at ease as I knew that he would receive the right treatment.

The two years in the centre were the most important years of Ibrahim's life. He started to mature and I could see signs that he was improving, although he was not overcoming all of his difficulties. All the tell tale signs suggested that Ibrahim had a semantic and pragmatic language disorder. He was not diagnosed with being autistic, although he had some autistic-like tendencies. The main indications were: the delay in the development of his language; remembering parts of a television programme and repeating phrases he heard from it (echolalia); difficulty in having a conversation and understanding all social situations. His condition had an effect on his behaviour and diet and almost every aspect of his life including his motor skills. Ibrahim was able to talk, but he was only able to manage phrases that he had previously learnt. It was difficult to try and make sense of the situation, but at least we now knew what we were dealing with.

Ibrahim did not find it easy to organise himself at home. In the mornings, I had to make sure he had everything he needed for the day. He was able to dress himself without assistance, but was very slow and needed prompting all the time. A common problem was that, while Ibrahim was half dressed, he would be distracted by something in his room, for example a toy, and would start to play with it, forgetting that he had to dress quickly for school. I was always forced to nag him repeatedly. Ibrahim did not like rushing in the mornings, but at times it was unavoidable. He would play imaginative games and be easily distracted by noises or movement of people and it took a considerable time for him to learn to speed up.

An example of Ibrahim's problems can be shown by an episode when he read *The Gingerbread Man* as part of his speech therapy sessions. He was told to retell the story while looking at the pictures. This is how Ibrahim told the story.

> "The old woman is making the gingerbread man and he's putting gingers on his body and putting on, put gingers on his eyes (interruption), and then he put and then he put and then the old woman puts a gingerbread man in the oven to bake and then he comes alive. The old woman says 'STOP' but he wanted to eat the gingerbread man ... He wants to go to the pond."

It is obvious from this passage that his problems were complex and included changes of tense, hesitation and word difficulties. He incorrectly named 'gingers' for 'currants' and 'pond' for 'river' and later in the story, Ibrahim talked about a cow as if it was a 'he' or 'she'.

During normal conversations, Ibrahim would hesitate whilst constructing sentences. He would always talk to himself, having quiet conversations and thinking aloud. His so-called quiet conversations were, however, loud enough for others to hear and he would isolate himself, withdrawing from everything that was going on around him. Once, while on a school trip, Ibrahim kept saying, 'Now back to the studio!' which was a phrase he had learnt from news programmes. His teacher, Kate Ivy, informed me of this, which we found quite amusing. Ibrahim's difficulties amused us in many different ways. With the serious side of his nature came an amusing side and this helped to lighten the situation a little.

At the centre, Ibrahim enjoyed having a visual timetable, which was displayed on the wall with the other children's, to remind them which activities they would be undertaking each day. He looked forward to studying his as it planned his day, which he found helpful. Ibrahim needed rules. Most children with speech and language difficulties need rules and without them Ibrahim was lost. He still had difficulties in socialising with his classmates. He would put his arm around other children's necks, unintentionally hurting them in the process. One thing that helped him in this area was the social skills training he received, which focused on listening to others, turn taking and appropriate/inappropriate behaviour. Although Ibrahim was able to understand what he had done wrong, he was still unable to transfer this knowledge to another situation.

Ibrahim found it difficult to understand and accept everyday situations. Any change of routine would make him upset and frustrated. He needed to be familiar with what he was about to do and at home he relied on me to guide him. At times he would play alone for hours and hours, not complaining that he was hungry or asking for something to eat because he was not interested in eating and was used to going without food almost for the whole day. His eating pattern also showed signs of a fixation with routine. As I have already mentioned, the only food he loved to eat was 'Linda McCartney's deep country pies'. He had these for months on end, until he became bored of them. There also came a time when I could not stand the sight of them!

I still had a problem persuading Ibrahim to eat at other people's homes. He would die of thirst rather than have a sip of his favourite drink, which was Coca Cola. This was always a problem, no matter how much I encouraged him; Ibrahim would not eat anywhere apart from his own home. I even tried to tempt him with toys and games, but it did not help the situation, even though at times I felt he wanted to but just could not. It was important that I always made sure he had something to eat before we went out anywhere as I knew his next meal wouldn't be until we returned home. This became very frustrating and I tried to avoid going out at mealtimes, or if we did, I made sure that we came back home on time for his meal. Although his appetite was small, it was important to stick to regular mealtimes.

When we used to visit my mother's house, I would sometimes cook for everyone or would just help my mother. I always made sure that Ibrahim knew that I was cooking so that he would eat the meal I prepared. He would say, 'Yes I'll eat it.' I always believed he would as he was very convincing, but sadly, when the time came, he would refuse to eat the food without giving a reason. He would just explain that he couldn't eat it. He followed the same pattern each time, assuring me that he would eat, only to change his mind at the last minute. I always believed him, thinking that this day would be the day that he would eat, but that day never seemed to come.

After many months, I gave up. I realised I had to stop myself from being pushy. Ibrahim's eating was a psychological matter. Something in his brain was not allowing him to eat and was telling him 'Don't eat!' Ibrahim refused to try new foods and he was extremely stubborn. Nothing I said or did would tempt him. He wouldn't even look at new foods and would leave the room if I asked him to try something new in case he was physically sick. Even the thought of trying new foods made him feel sick, and I had to allow him to improve his eating in his own time, which meant I had to be very patient. When we went visiting friends' or relatives' homes, Ibrahim was always offered a drink and perhaps a snack. Usually, I made excuses to people saying that he was not hungry, but after a while this excuse wore thin. Ibrahim was known in our family for not eating at other peoples' houses and they found it hard to believe that he ate anything at all; it was difficult to convince even the closest relative that I was not intentionally starving him.

Ibrahim was invited to a friend's birthday party in April 1997. It was the first invitation to a party that he had had. He had not been invited to a party before, as he never made any real friends. He did not interact with children appropriately and because of this, he was not regarded as a friend to them. The invitation came from a boy called Oliver who was also a pupil in the speech and language unit. At his age, Ibrahim did not understand the meaning of a birthday party. We did have a couple of parties for Ibrahim when he was younger and I remember once Ibrahim would not join in and played happily in a quiet room all on his own. He was not interested, despite being shown all his presents, and even when it was time to blow the candles on the cake, he was still not impressed.

The day of the party arrived. At first, when he entered Oliver's house, he refused to say hello to Oliver or his parents. He just ran inside to the toys that were in the hall and started to play with them. He did not play with the other children, but fortunately Oliver's parents were aware of Ibrahim's difficulties so they knew what to expect. Most children will have something to eat at parties, but not Ibrahim. He would only drink Coca Cola, and the only food he ate was a chocolate cup cake. However, I viewed this small feat as a breakthrough and I was very pleased about this. It may have only been a cup cake, but at least he ate something, however small. I was told his eating would improve through maturity and gradually it did with much perseverance.

Ibrahim had many obsessions throughout his life and Thomas the Tank Engine was one of them. I bought him a Thomas the Tank Engine bag and books; my sister bought him videos, t-shirts, a lunch box and beaker. For his sixth birthday his uncle gave him a Thomas train set which he still gets lots of enjoyment from today. Ibrahim watched the videos over and over again and never became tired of them. He had watched them so many times that he knew most of the stories off by heart. He would repeat dialogue from the videos when he would play with his Thomas trains. I did not mind as I felt it was not doing Ibrahim any harm, however, it was difficult encouraging him to watch other videos.

Ibrahim found it difficult to pour a glass of milk properly without spilling some outside the glass. It was difficult for him to hold something steady and he would accidentally drop drinks from his hands. Unfortunately, this would happen far too often. Once, without telling me, Ibrahim decided to pour himself a glass of milk.

Somehow, he dropped the carton and there was a big puddle of milk on the kitchen floor. Ibrahim probably expected me to get cross, but I managed to restrain myself, as I knew that he tried to be independent and pour it properly. I told him it did not matter and felt very sorry for him. It took a lot of practice before he mastered this task. After dropping many glasses of milk and coke, I can now confirm that he is now able to pour a drink without dropping it.

Another problem Ibrahim had was the habit of tripping himself up, falling over and bumping into things. When we walked in the street, he would walk behind me and sometimes would virtually walk on top of me or bump into me, even when we walked in a straight line. I had to constantly tell him to move away, so that I would have enough room to walk. He had help with this at the centre to enable him to leave space in front of him when he was walking and this improved matters. However, even today, he still has this problem and he does not find it easy to allow space around him.

By this time, Ibrahim was learning to ride a bicycle with stabilizers. He was able to do this but fell off a lot even when he rode in a straight line. It was noticeable that Ibrahim had difficulties with his legs. Although he was able to walk, run and jump, something did not look quite right. He was also very thin for his age, although his height was about average. His arms were noticeably long, especially his fingers. When doing things, he would find it difficult to bend his fingers and relax them. They were always kept straight and it was as though he was afraid to bend them. One could see by looking at his finger actions that there was something wrong. At times, when I held something in my hand to give to Ibrahim, for instance, a coin, I would have expected him to hold out his hand for me to place it in his palm. However, he would grasp it with all of his long, slender fingers in a snatching motion. I soon realised that we had to practise how to hold things and how to take objects from someone in the correct manner. Most children would naturally do this without needing any extra coaching, but Ibrahim seemed to keep his fingers so straight that he hardly bent them. We practised how

35

to relax his fingers and bend them when necessary. This was part of his on-going difficulties with his gross and fine motor skills. After a lot of frustration and upset we got there in the end. Ibrahim also found it difficult making models with shapes and sticking together small boxes and he needed a lot of exercises to strengthen his hand muscles.

Ibrahim's poor co-ordination made him look weak, clumsy and vulnerable. Ibrahim was not particularly good at running, but he was able to run in a fashion which was quite slow. All sports were a struggle for him no matter how hard he tried. For example, Ibrahim was unable to kick a ball in a straight line, but he enjoyed the exercise even though he found things hard going.

Simple things like holding a knife and fork proved difficult for him. He was unable to hold them in the usual manner and even today he still finds it hard. He holds a fork with his left hand and uses it as if he was stabbing something. Ibrahim also finds it difficult to spoon something properly without dropping some of the contents. I have demonstrated to him many times how to hold them correctly, but he finds it difficult to copy someone in this way. Sitting still at meal times was another problem. He just could not sit still at all, even on the bus or in the car. If he did sit down, he would fiddle with the nearest object to him, bang on the chair he was sitting on or bang on the wall as if he was playing a tune he knew. He is still very fidgety today and this can be very irritating at times. I think most of the time he does not realise he is doing it, so I have to constantly remind him to stop.

Ibrahim was unable to predict things. He could not even try to imagine what could happen in a particular situation. I once asked him what would happen if he ran around with a drink in his hand, but he was not able to tell me. Something had to actually occur for him to understand the situation, but the same circumstances could occur again and again and he still would not be able to tell me. This reminds me of goldfish – they eat food, forget that they have just eaten something and eat again; this manifests itself to overeating. The cycle goes on and on. This is quite similar to Ibrahim's situation – he would do something he is not supposed to do, be told not to do it again, then he would forget and would do it again. I always asked him if he could remember the last time he did this; he always replied that he could not remember. The whole cycle would repeat itself, again and again. At times, I would feel fed up with repeating things, but it was something I had to do in order to teach Ibrahim ...

For the first time, Ibrahim's uncle took him to the cinema to watch Star Wars – Episode One. We decided to do this as an experiment to see how he would react. We were confident that he would be able to sit through the film without any major difficulties. I was quite excited with the thought that he was now able to go to the cinema, just like other children his age. Sadly, our expectations of him were wrong, as Ibrahim's uncle reported that he was very fidgety and was unable to sit still. He was also loud in expressing his happiness in some scenes. He found it amazing to watch a film on a big screen and, during one scene; he stood up and said, 'Yes!' after the Death Star exploded. Ibrahim did not realise that you are not supposed to shout at the cinema and that you should sit quietly as there were other people watching the film too. Ibrahim was thirsty during the film, but his uncle explained that it was best not to have a drink, as he would need the toilet. Surprise, surprise, after his uncle relented and got him a drink, Ibrahim needed the toilet, which his uncle found annoying. It was only later that we discovered that Ibrahim only wanted to go to the toilet so that he could buy another drink from the drinks machine, because he was fascinated by them. This shows that Ibrahim had a manipulative side to him also. We decided that it would be best if Ibrahim did not go to the cinema for a while until he was mature enough to understand.

A common problem with Ibrahim was interacting appropriately with other children. In April 1997, Ibrahim's cousin came over to play. He was a few months older than Ibrahim and they decided to play football on the green just at the rear of our house. After a while Ibrahim's cousin had had enough and decided to head home, but Ibrahim was keen to continue playing and could not accept the fact that the game was now over. Ibrahim punched his cousin, as I watched from a distance. His cousin came home quite upset and told me what had happened. I asked Ibrahim why he punched him. He replied, 'He didn't want to play anymore.' Ibrahim always expected other children to play by his rules and always liked to be in control of situations. We talked about how wrong it was and I was very concerned about his cousin telling his mother and they would think Ibrahim was a violent, naughty boy.

I spoke to his teacher about this violent behaviour, as it was a regular occurrence and I needed advice on how to deal with the situation. His teacher advised that I should draw out the scene, as pictures do help a child understand things better than words. I did this and talked about the situation, discussing what he should have done and what he should do next time. No matter how many times we would talk about this, Ibrahim would not be able to apply it in the heat of the moment. It was difficult for him to learn rules and then apply them to the situation, and I knew this would take time to come. All my dealings with Ibrahim invariably required time, patience and effort.

CHAPTER 5

A NEW MEMBER OF THE FAMILY

In May 1997, Ibrahim's brother, Imran, was born. There was now a new member of the family. Ibrahim woke up on the 23rd May to find his aunt sleeping in the bed next to his and neither myself nor his father at home. Due to the circumstances, he did not go to school that day. His aunt explained that he had a new brother and they were going to visit him at the hospital that morning. I did not worry at all about being apart from Ibrahim because I knew my sister would take good care of him and he was very close to her.

When Ibrahim came to see Imran for the first time, he cried, showing what a very sensitive boy he was. His interest in Imran only lasted for just a few minutes until he turned to me and said how much he missed me. After a further fifteen minutes, Ibrahim's attention turned to the coffee machine, which he remembered passing on his way in to see us. He demanded a hot chocolate drink, so his dad let him have one, but Ibrahim managed to drop the whole drink on the floor. He was also inquisitive about other things around the hospital, not realising the sole purpose of the visit was to see his baby brother for the first time.

One thing that sticks in my mind about this whole episode is the effect that Imran had on Ibrahim. Every time he looked at Imran, he became tearful and when Imran cried, this upset him even more. Ibrahim also became emotional when he looked at his own baby photographs and we had to hide them so that he would not be able to find them. Anything to do with babies seemed to upset him for some inexplicable reason.

Gradually, Ibrahim's jealousy towards Imran began to show. Ibrahim had been the only child until now and he had always had our complete and undivided attention. Now that attention had to be shared with Imran and I realised I had to be extra vigilant when they were both together. Ibrahim was keen on touching Imran's soft spot on his scalp, which was a little worrying. I always invited Ibrahim to help me with nappy changing and bathing, so that he would not feel left out. I think this helped him to realise that things were a lot different now.

Knowing how difficult Ibrahim could be, I worried about the effect that a new member of the family would have on his behaviour. His mood swings continually affected our lives and he was difficult to keep amused, thinking the world revolved around him. We didn't want the situation to worsen because Ibrahim was struggling enough already. Other members of the family, especially his aunt, made him feel special. My sister was very discerning and she was well aware that it was important that Ibrahim felt happy and secure now that Imran was part of the family.

Ibrahim could focus his attention on an activity for about thirty minutes now, which was a big improvement. The quality of his concentration varied and Ibrahim found it difficult to transfer skills he had learnt in one to one situations to small group activities. It was a completely different scenario for him and he seemed to be completely lost. His eye contact varied and everything hinged on how he was feeling on any given day. If he was tired, he would switch off and become uncommunicative. If he was overworking, he would become confused and upset and his mind would go blank. This would show in his facial expression and it would be evident for all to see.

In a speech therapy session, Ibrahim was assessed in a one to one situation. He was shown a picture of a girl patting a dog. When asked to describe the scene, he said, 'There's a girl whose got a dog and he's got a long tail and four feet and fur on and the girl is eight years old.' Another picture showed a girl trying to put a large parcel in a post box. When asked why she found it difficult, Ibrahim said, ' Because you can't put one inside it because it's got a line on it – you have to take it to Parcel Force.' He interpreted a boy hitting a ball with a pan as, 'He's panning the ball.' All these examples clearly show the difficulties he had in choosing appropriate words and the way he invented new words such as 'panning'. It highlighted the severity of his speech and language disorder and how trying to interpret simple pictures was difficult for him. He even found it difficult talking about a television programme he had just watched. Recounting stories would just confuse him and describing something briefly was very difficult for him. He was unable to find the right words and needed a lot of help with this aspect of his development.

Ibrahim had difficulties with his imagination. He was unable to create stories and was unable to distinguish between reality and fantasy. This was especially evident when he read stories. Once Ibrahim read the well-known story, *The Tiger Who Came To Tea*. His teacher asked him, 'Do real tigers eat cake?' Ibrahim replied, 'No they eat sandwiches.' Where on earth he got this from, I really don't know. It was as if he felt compelled to give an answer, even if the answer was incorrect. We had to go through the story at home explaining that tigers live in the wild and are dangerous and they would not come to tea. It was just a fantasy story for children to enjoy. I also tried to make him understand that if he was unsure about something, he could ask his teacher rather than say the first thing that came into his head. Ibrahim seemed happy with my explanation, but I knew he would need reminding again each time a similar situation arose.

Despite his difficulties with imagination, Ibrahim was excellent at reading with expression. He gradually developed the ability to read a story to me exactly in the style it was read to him. He could retell Thomas the Tank Engine stories he had seen on video exactly in the way it was narrated. Ibrahim has loved books since he was very young and is still an excellent reader and this is one of his greatest achievements. He has never found reading difficult and has always enjoyed it, which is something I am proud of. His reading age has always been advanced for his years and because of this, Ibrahim's problems have been disguised and it can appear as if there is nothing wrong with him.

Ibrahim's gross and fine motor skills were always classified as abnormal. However, they were gradually improving with the exercises he was given at the centre, for example, cutting shapes, painting, gluing objects together and modelling shapes with plasticine. However, his drawings had little shape and form and he always found drawing difficult and tried to avoid doing it. This was one of his weaker points, but I never pushed him to draw. I didn't like to make him do something he did not like doing, otherwise it would lead to frustration and resentment. Ibrahim also had problems with applying knowledge and in problem solving. For instance, in maths, he found it difficult to understand more abstract concepts involved in weight and capacity. During one exercise, he was able to count how many small containers of water it took to fill a large container, but was unsure which of them could hold more water.

Eventually, Ibrahim was able to write the entire alphabet correctly, but he asserted so much pressure with his pencil that an indent was clearly seen on the page underneath. At times, the lead in his pencil broke, and his teachers would comment that Ibrahim needed to correct his pencil grip as he held it in a peculiar way. Ibrahim used all of his fingers to hold a pencil rather than holding it in the traditional manner, and he still holds a pencil in the same way today. By the end of year one, July 1997, Ibrahim was able to add and subtract numbers up to twenty. Mechanical maths was easier for him than problem solving, but he still found the language of maths quite difficult and needed a lot of assistance in this area.

CHAPTER 6

THE SADDEST TIME OF OUR LIVES

On a fine evening on 15 August 1997, Ibrahim's aunt came over to our house with her husband. Our next-door neighbour's little girl, Alice, also came over to play. She came to play with Ibrahim almost every day and Ibrahim enjoyed having someone to play with. When my sister arrived, Alice wanted to go home and asked to be escorted. Ibrahim wanted to take her and my sister decided to go with them, but Ibrahim did not want this. He demanded to go on his own with Alice, but she decided that she would rather have my sister take her home. Ibrahim started to sulk and became very moody. When my sister returned home, he completely ignored her and showed his grievance with her by sulking. He didn't even say goodbye to her when she went home, all this because she took Alice home. This was typical of how Ibrahim would overreact to certain situations, even things as apparently unimportant as escorting Alice home. Once he had started to sulk, it was difficult to reason with him and it was better simply to leave him alone.

The next morning, I received a phone call from my mother telling me that my sister was feeling very ill and an ambulance was on its way. I was worried and decided to go to my sister's house, with Ibrahim and Imran. When we arrived, the ambulance had just left so my brother, mother and I together with the children headed for the hospital. At the hospital, we waited in the corridor for what seemed like ages. Ibrahim became very impatient and I was not in the mood to keep him amused. One of my cousins came and took

Ibrahim back to his house, as it was felt that the hospital was not the ideal place for him to be. Unfortunately, my sister passed away about thirty minutes after they had left. This was a great shock for my family. She apparently had an underlying heart problem, but nobody expected this to happen. I was heartbroken as I went to collect Ibrahim from my cousin's house. Ibrahim looked at me and said, 'Is she in heaven now?' I was relieved by this remark. At least he knew without me having to break the news. I would have found it very difficult to tell him because of the emotional state I was in. Someone he had become very close to was now gone, yet Ibrahim only seemed to show emotion because everyone else was upset. This was the most difficult time in Ibrahim's life so far. He became a little withdrawn and quiet and regretted the way he behaved when he saw her for the last time. I told him that he was not to know this would happen and it did not mean that she loved him any less. Unlike the rest of the family, Ibrahim still has tears in his eyes when we talk about her. With the passage of time, we can talk about her without being tearful, but Ibrahim is still unable to do this.

Ibrahim went to the funeral as I felt this would help him understand the finality of death and where his aunt was now. In hindsight, it was not the right thing to do as the funeral upset him further. He was struggling to come to terms with what was happening because it all occurred very suddenly. We were all struggling in different ways, and Ibrahim desperately wanted to know why this had happened. Whatever I said left his questions unanswered. This tragedy taught Ibrahim that we have to accept what comes in our lives and that not everything goes according to plan. Ibrahim already had difficulties understanding everyday situations, and a tragedy like this put a greater burden on him. Ibrahim needed the security of knowing what was going to happen and when.

I talked to him about what had happened and I tried not to show emotion in his presence. As the months passed, I found it easier to talk to Ibrahim and discuss things with him in general. He seemed to be maturing and it appeared that he was at a turning point in his life, as if he had begun to turn the corner towards making great progress. However, this did not mean that his problems had gone away – there were other areas of his development that needed concentrating on.

Ibrahim still needed a lot of prompting and reminding to do things all the time. It was necessary to remind him about the same things day after day for weeks on end, but he still could not remember to do them without being prompted by me. I became tired of telling him to do the same things over and over again, but without reminding him, he would be lost. He needed constant guidance in order to feel confident in everyday situations.

It seems strange to think that Ibrahim was still drinking milk from a baby's bottle until the age of five. I found it very difficult weaning him off it as he found it soothing and would go to sleep with it. I remember one time when he demanded to take his bottle with him when we went shopping, so we had to. A woman in a shop commented to her friend, 'That boy still drinks from a bottle!' She seemed shocked by this and I felt awful and embarrassed. Then one day, Ibrahim's bottle cracked when it fell on the floor. I threw it away and promised myself that was it, no more bottles, and I didn't give him one again. He complained about it for a few days, but then stopped. He found it difficult to suck from a straw, even though most children start before the age of two. Ibrahim could not drink from a cup on his own and it took a very long time for him to learn. There was the added problem of his clumsiness. He would regularly drop drinks on the floor and it took a long time for him to be able to hold his cup steady. This was all to do with his poor gross and fine motor skills, but he always tried very hard and I always gave him praise to encourage him to improve.

CHAPTER 7

'WHY CAN'T HE BE NORMAL?'

Ibrahim's problems had a huge impact on the family, but mostly on me. There were bad days when I would think, 'Why can't he be normal? Why did it happen to my family?' On a good day, it didn't seem to matter so much and I coped well. However, sometimes I felt under great pressure and it was all too easy to lose my temper over small things. I realised I had to learn to be patient the hard way. I would forget that the mistakes Ibrahim made were because of his problems and that it was not his fault, and everything become an enormous strain. The pressure caused me to feel quite depressed at times and I became quite tearful. The prospect of having to struggle everyday in this way was demoralising and I wasn't sure I could cope.

I was only 22 years old when we discovered that Ibrahim had difficulties. Life seemed so unfair to burden me like this at an age when I was still young and inexperienced. The normal everyday things that most people do with their children were major stressful situations for me. I was also spending a great deal of time and effort trying to make my own family understand Ibrahim's difficulties and I didn't realise the strain it was putting on me. I used to lie awake late at night trying to find answers to my questions and I had a good cry at times. I felt isolated and alone, and this isolation was exacerbated when I no longer had my sister to talk to. She always had time for me when we talked about Ibrahim, but talking about Ibrahim's problems did not make them disappear.

Only much later did I realise that Ibrahim's language difficulties would be a long-term problem. It was something I needed to learn to understand and cope with so that we could get on with life as best we could. Life was not going to stop or slow down because we wanted it to. It was important to remember the good points and that Ibrahim achieved many things and was able to do things that other children his age were not able to do. For example, his reading ability was advanced for his age and this was something I was very proud of. In the midst of all my problems, it was easy to forget his good points.

By the end of 1997, Ibrahim was reading Arabic fluently. He attended a school on Saturdays which he had done since the age of five, and he enjoyed this very much. Ibrahim watched Quranic videos, in which verses of the Quran were read in Arabic, slowly and clearly. He enjoyed watching these videos and managed to memorize verses without too much difficulty. What was unusual was that he learnt to read Arabic through these videos which most children do not do. It seemed as if Ibrahim's reading just happened. He learnt in his own way quickly and easily, which was unusual because Arabic is not an easy language to learn.

By the age of seven and a half, Ibrahim could manage to read the whole of the Quran in Arabic. At this age, the majority of children are only just starting to read a few words and I was at least twelve before I managed to master the Quran. It was amazing that, despite Ibrahim's language difficulties, he was able to read in another language and learnt through watching videos. His Arabic accent was excellent too, which was another great achievement and I was very proud of him. It is sad that these amazing feats hid the fact that he had language difficulties and made it more difficult for people to understand his problems.

Bengali was spoken at home, but Ibrahim still found this language difficult to speak correctly because the language structure is different to that of English. I felt that it was important for him to learn the language, however little, so that he was able to communicate with other members of the family who were not so good at

47

speaking English, including his nana. Learning three languages at the same time put even more pressure on him, but Ibrahim coped extremely well despite the difficulties he had.

Around the beginning of 1998, when Ibrahim was seven years old, his concentration was more controlled. He could now apply himself for about five minutes without getting distracted. This may not sound much of an accomplishment, but it was a big achievement for Ibrahim considering his difficulties. Distractions complicated everything for Ibrahim and he therefore needed a quiet environment to be able to concentrate on his work. At school, there were always many things happening at the same time and this caused him to be distracted. He was now able to work for up to half an hour without needing a break, but he needed constant reminders to refocus in class sessions.

I always welcomed feedback from his school so that I could be kept up to date on Ibrahim's progress. His school report stated that he found it difficult to concentrate on what was being shown to him on school trips because he wanted to move on to the next item very swiftly. This was also a problem at home. He didn't want to absorb the content of what he was doing and before giving himself a chance, he wanted to move on to something else.

When it came to socialising with people, Ibrahim found it difficult to focus on what other people were saying. In group discussions he would distract himself and others by talking about irrelevant topics for the sake of making conversation. He was such a chatterbox! He didn't have difficulty making speech sounds, but he did have a tendency to mumble when talking at length and lacked clarity of ideas. He spoke in a quiet voice and I sometimes found it difficult to catch what he was saying. There was an improvement in his story telling compared to the previous year. On one occasion he recounted the story of *The Great Big Enormous Turnip* on tape to a Learning Support Assistant, which was part of his Statutory Review Assessment. Ibrahim was told to retell the story in his own words whilst looking at the pictures with the words covered up. This is how he told the story:

And then the old man and the old woman and the granddaughter and the dog pull the turnip but they couldn't pull it up.

And then the dog calls for the cat but the cat is cross.

And then the cat calls for the mouse but the mouse is a bit frightened of the cat because the cat wants to eat the mouse.

And then the old man, the old woman, the granddaughter and the dog and the cat and the mouse pulled together and then they pulled it up.

And then they caught it at last and they all rolled over. And then they have it for dinner.

In this retelling, Ibrahim was able to give a clear narrative without the hesitations, which were very apparent in his story telling in the previous year. Ibrahim's understanding and use of individual words had improved although he changed tense several times, which was common for a child of his age. He still found expressive language very difficult. When his teacher had told the story to his class, Ibrahim remembered how she had described the animals' feelings and he was able to use the same words in his retelling. However, when asked a question which had not been discussed in class, he was unable to provide a satisfactory answer. For example, when asked to attribute a motive for the cat, the conversation went like this:

LSA: 'What does he do?'
Ibrahim: 'He calls for the old woman.'
LSA: 'What's she doing?'
Ibrahim's: 'Feeding her parrot.'
LSA: 'What's the cat doing?'
Ibrahim: 'Looking at the parrot.'
LSA: 'Why do you think he's looking at the parrot?'
Ibrahim: 'Er, don't know.'

Ibrahim's use of pronouns was improving but he still had difficulties with the more complex ones and his language difficulties continued to have an impact on his learning. At school, during a therapy session, Ibrahim was trying to ascertain who liked eating raisins. His class teacher asked his speech therapist whether she liked them. Ibrahim said 'Yes.' His teacher asked him how he knew and he answered, 'Because she likes them and because she's eating them,' which she was not. It took a great deal of prompting for him to realise that he could have found out simply by asking. This highlights how at times he failed to see what was obvious to the rest of us.

Ibrahim was confident enough to answer questions in school assemblies. He didn't mind putting his hand up to speak and he wasn't phased when the other children turned around to look at him. I remember when I was at school I was too shy to answer questions in class. I used to dread being chosen and I was too frightened to put my hand up. I was pleased that Ibrahim enjoyed being chosen. Every time he had answered up in assembly, it was the first thing he would tell me about straight after school. His face would glow with delight and it was very important to him. This was the start of Ibrahim's new-found confidence. His ability to answer straightforward questions related to the text was also improving, although it was still inconsistent.

Ibrahim's vocabulary was now excellent for his age and was well above average. At the age of seven years and two months, Ibrahim had a spelling age of ten. He was keen to learn new vocabulary all the time and we provided him with a dictionary – *The Oxford Primary School Dictionary and Thesaurus*. He spent many hours looking up new words and always liked to tell me about them, many of which I had never heard of. His writing was beginning to make more sense and his construction of sentences was improving. Verbal communication had always been a problem for him before and it had been difficult to understand exactly what he was saying, so this was indeed a milestone. He was now making good progress in all areas which was a huge relief.

Ibrahim was now starting to understand the concept of money. He could add coins together to the value of one pound. He found this useful when we went shopping and he helped me calculate the cost of the shopping, but he found it difficult to understand why we were given change when we bought things. I knew it would take a little longer for him to understand this, but I was confident he would get there eventually. He was starting to understand time, which was another good thing. This enabled him to grasp the concept of 'later on' and he was able to plan things he could do later. I was happy with the progress Ibrahim was making, although I knew we still had a long way to go.

CHAPTER 8

FURTHER PROGRESS

Between 1997 and 1998, Ibrahim matured into a more sensible boy. This was the most important time of Ibrahim's life so far. He was integrating more into Year 2 class for reading, although he still spent the rest of the time at the centre.

Physically hurting the other children in his class was happening less often, although it had not ceased altogether. For example, he would sometimes try to exclude another member of the class from the game he was playing. I knew I had to be patient. He had made such marvellous progress, but there were bound to be areas he still needed to work on. Ibrahim was now starting to show some responsibility. It had been his normal pattern to be quick to ask for help before he had given himself the chance to understand things. Now he had to learn a balance between two extremes of either never asking for clarification or being entirely dependent on the teacher.

At home he was always dependent on me, although I knew he was able to do many things independently. I tried to encourage Ibrahim to work out simple instructions for himself, but he seemed afraid to do this in case he got things wrong. He wanted to get everything right the first time. I would ask him to do simple tasks for me at home, such as fetching something for me from the bathroom. He would ask me several times what I had asked him to do, going through the instructions again and again with me. It took so long for him to perform the simplest of tasks that I may as well have fetched it myself. I felt it was more effort than what it was worth and, after a few negative experiences, I stopped asking him to do me favours. I thought that I may have been expecting too much from him and he needed more time.

At times, Ibrahim would do some cooking at school with his class. He made some biscuits one day and bought them home after school, telling me he did not want to eat them. I tried to encourage him to eat a small nibble, but he stubbornly refused. Another time, when Ibrahim made a fresh-fruit salad, he was the only child in his class who refused to try it. This became a common occurrence. When it came to eating fruit, we had another battle on our hands because he refused to eat any type of fruit. He wouldn't even look at fruit, never mind try it. I did not try to force him, even though he had eaten it quite happily as a baby. I felt it was a shame that he was missing out on such an important part of his diet but, once again, there was little I could do but be patient.

My patience finally paid off. On one occasion at school during his speech and language group, he made sandwiches. When he came home from school, he ate them! He had not eaten them before and this was the first ever sandwich he had eaten at home. Ibrahim told me he preferred to eat grated cheese sandwiches with butter on the bread. I was so pleased that a new food had been incorporated into his diet. Later, I introduced him to lettuce and he then preferred to have cheese and lettuce sandwiches. This may seem insignificant to most mothers, but this small breakthrough in his diet meant so much to me. As Ibrahim's appetite and choice of foods improved, he began to have school dinners, but still he did not eat everything. Eventually Ibrahim started to eat cheeseburgers as long as the burger contained lettuce and cheese with nothing else. He did not like chips even though all children love chips. It would take a long time for Ibrahim to develop a liking for most foods, and I knew that his fussiness would not disappear altogether but would be life-long.

Ibrahim was given a book to take home so that I could add comments regarding his progress or areas of concern. It was a good way of communicating with his teachers about things that occurred at home and at school or to highlight any worries I may have regarding Ibrahim. It was rare for me to see the teachers, so I saw it as a good way of keeping in touch. I had to log in the book all the things we had done at the weekend and Ibrahim was asked about the events at school to help him with his expressive language.

From March 1998 he was able to write his own news, which he enjoyed very much. There was a great improvement in his handwriting, although it took him rather a long time to write a few sentences. Ibrahim was now learning to do joined-up writing, which initially looked very messy. It became neater with practise and he could now use full stops, question marks, exclamation marks and commas appropriately in his writing. He still asserted a lot of pressure with his pen on the paper which slowed him down so much that he hardly ever completed a piece of work at school. He did not like to leave his work unfinished so he knew he had to learn to write faster, but this would come as his gross and fine motor skills improved.

Ibrahim became obsessed with *Robot Wars* on television. This is a programme where teams build robots which then go into battle, rather like gladiators preparing for combat. The winner was the robot that could upturn or halt the opposing robot. Ibrahim enjoyed the battles and rough play and he never missed an episode. If ever the worst happened and he did miss his favourite programme, he felt that his day was incomplete and he moped around for the rest of the evening. Once we went out and I recorded an episode for him to watch later. Ibrahim complained bitterly about this because he had always been able to watch it when it was broadcast live on television at the same time every week. He knew exactly when it was on, despite not being familiar with time, and *Robot Wars* was part of his life. He isolated himself from the rest of the world when he was watching it, which was very annoying at times. I allowed him to watch it because I didn't think it would do him any harm. I believed it was a phase he was going through and I was sure he would become bored of it eventually.

Ibrahim played *Robot Wars* with his toy cars. Each car was given a name and he would pretend that he was having a contest with them, taking it all really seriously. He would even commentate, which he did very loudly in the same manner and style as the presenter in the actual television programme. This went on for months and Ibrahim joined the *Robot Wars* club, receiving newsletters and a pin badge, which he loved. It was only a matter of time before his focus of attention was drawn elsewhere. Ibrahim always had difficulty in playing age appropriate imaginative games.

Ibrahim's social skills were also visibly improving. However, he still had difficulties in understanding other peoples' feelings. He would say things that other children found hurtful and he also said things that you shouldn't say to people. I had to teach him to be tactful and not be rude to people when we were out. There were times, however, when he would show empathy towards people and his eye contact was improving. This is an important part of his social skills and it took a long time for Ibrahim to realise that he had to look at someone when they talked to him or when he was talking to them. To see him making such improvements was truly amazing and I was so proud of him.

Comprehension was still an area Ibrahim was struggling with. I helped him at home with his schoolwork and Ibrahim's speech and language centre sent books home for him to read. I set questions for him to practise his comprehension skills every week. We also talked about the books and the pictures, which helped him greatly. To highlight the difficulties Ibrahim had with comprehension, there was one time at school when he read a story about a frog and toad. Frog sent toad a letter by giving it to a snail to deliver. The text read, 'Four days later it arrived.' The teacher asked how long the snail took to deliver the letter. Ibrahim answered, 'Fifty minutes.' How he arrived at this answer and what he was thinking at the time I really don't know and I don't think he knew either.

Ibrahim spent a lot of time at his nana's house and it became his second home. We went there regularly every weekend and Ibrahim learnt how to play snooker there and played regularly with one of his uncles. Playing snooker helped his hand-eye co-ordination and concentration and it taught him to hold things steadily, which he was not particularly good at. Ibrahim's hand was always shaky when he tried to pot a ball. However, this got better in time and his highest break was twenty-seven and over time he was able to pot balls quite accurately.

One day Ibrahim went to town with his uncle and new aunty. They decided to walk even though it was raining. On the way home, Ibrahim demanded to have an ice cream. He was not normally allowed ice creams because he took too long to eat them and this made such a mess. His uncle thought it was not an appropriate time for him to be eating anyway, and he refused to let him have one. Typically, Ibrahim threw a tantrum all the way home, and they found him extremely difficult to handle. They reported back that Ibrahim had not listened to them and had been very naughty. I was very disappointed to hear this and had hoped for much more, considering his recent improvements. It was so easy to expect too much and forget that Ibrahim could behave in this manner and it was at times like this when I felt very low. Again, I blamed myself. I should have known this would happen; I should not have allowed this to happen; I was at fault. I felt so guilty because I desperately wanted everyone to think well of Ibrahim.

When Ibrahim played games such as Connect Four, he liked to record the score. There always had to be a points system otherwise the game was incomplete for him, and he used a calculator when necessary and wrote the scores down on paper. I would often find bits of paper scattered about the house with scores written down. Ibrahim enjoyed playing with other people and every time we had guests, Ibrahim would eagerly ask if anyone wanted to play a board game with him. He was more sociable with guests who came to our house if they were willing to play board games. Board games are a marvellous means of breaking down barriers for those with learning or communication difficulties. You are on equal terms with your opponent and you feel that, for once, the odds are even. Playing games was a language Ibrahim and his family understood together and it required little talk, which suited him fine.

Ibrahim was able to play quiz games on the teletext on television. It helped him build up his general knowledge. However, as with other games, he always had to win and if he lost he would become upset and play again and again until he won the game. He always wanted to be in control of everything, especially the games he played, and I think this made him feel secure. It took Ibrahim a long time to understand that he couldn't always expect to win games. There always had to be a winner and a loser, but Ibrahim could not accept being the latter. He would have to learn to control his emotions and try to understand the whole concept of game playing. This caused Ibrahim a great deal of upset rather than providing enjoyment. I hardly ever played board games with him, perhaps because I ended up doing everything else with him. He always complained about this, but I just was not interested and far too busy doing other things.

Ibrahim still found it difficult doing PE at school. Hopping, throwing and catching were particularly troublesome activities for him and a few children teased him about this. They would ignorantly call him a weakling, because he was so thin and struggled with simple action games. Even small tasks that most people find easy to do were frustrating for him. For example, attaching paper clips to hold papers together would take Ibrahim a long time. He found it difficult to be able to take things from the hands of other people. As I have already mentioned, if someone held out some coins for him to take, instead of holding out his hand, palm open, he would try to grasp them with his long fingers. I had to teach him these skills, which took many hours of practice and patience. Ibrahim only learnt to tie shoelaces at the age of ten!

At school, Ibrahim never really had a best friend like most children do. However, although he was quite popular with other children in the mainstream school, he tended to congregate with the group from the speech and language centre. He found it easier to interact with them as they had similar difficulties and they were mostly boys. Ibrahim became close to a boy called Marley, who had a severe speech disorder. Ibrahim seemed to enjoy watching out for him because he liked to be in control of situations, so that he would not feel lost or insecure in what he was doing. Ibrahim liked rules because they helped him to focus and guided him in a particular situation. Without a set of rules to follow, he would struggle with even the most basic of tasks.

In May 1998, it was decided that Ibrahim should take the SATS (standard assessment tests) at Key Stage One. He achieved Level 2 for English in reading, writing and comprehension tests, but only Level 1 in speaking and listening, which was not a surprise as most of his difficulties were in these areas. Ibrahim's spelling was excellent and he achieved Level 3 in the spelling test. In Mathematics, Ibrahim gained Level 2, which was an excellent achievement, as he had found Mathematics rather difficult to understand without a lot of assistance. He was assessed as Level 1 in Science, which was his weakest subject and one he found difficult to understand properly. Ibrahim had always worked hard, despite being under a great deal of pressure with the added problems of his disability. It was good to see that all the hard work and dedication the teachers had put in to help Ibrahim had paid off. They were very patient and understanding.

I have already explained that Ibrahim had a love of computers during his time at nursery school, but it did not stop there. By the age of eight, Ibrahim was able to switch on a computer, load the printer, save his work on the word processing program, print his work and shut down the computer when he was finished. He was very quick too and he was able to handle data on the computer to produce bar and pie charts. He seemed to relate to computers well and it was a totally new language for him which he was able to understand without having to speak it. From a very young age, Ibrahim has been fascinated with computers and I think this will last throughout his life.

In November 1998, an Educational Psychologist assessed Ibrahim on the Wechsler Scales in literacy and numeracy skills. His scores were as follows:

	Standard scores	Age equivalent
Basic reading	127	11 years 3 months
Spelling	139	14 years
Reading comprehension	103	8 years
Mathematical reasoning	111	8 years 6 months
Numerical operations	113	8 years 6 months

At the time of taking this test, Ibrahim was 7 years 10 months. In these results, the standard scores are based on a mean of 100, with the average scores being between 85 and 115. If you look at the chart, you will see that Ibrahim's scores were all either within or above the average range.

Ibrahim was able to spell unusual or difficult words often misspelled by adults, such as the word 'apparently', because of his use of his visual memory. However, in reading comprehension, he found it hard to translate text that he had just read and would prefer to reread the text rather than use his imagination, which suggested he had a low level of understanding. He was unable to make predictions and would give incorrect definitions to relatively easy words, but he was able to give correct responses to harder words.

Ibrahim continued to have difficulties with pragmatic and semantic aspects of language, which was still evident in his behaviour. His personality affected his behaviour in different ways and I believe this is the case with all children who experience language difficulties. He had problems in understanding other peoples' points of view, and using language to communicate subtly with non-verbal communication. In social situations for example, within the small group in the unit, he tended to be controlling and rather dominating. Ibrahim found it difficult to understand the facial expressions of other people, for instance, if they were unhappy. His understanding of both written and spoken information and receptive language was still an area of particular difficulty for him. He also had problems with open-ended social situations, which require understanding of another point of view or which require imagination or empathy and he struggled with social problem solving. Reading fictional stories had always been problematic for Ibrahim because he did not easily become imaginatively involved. Relating stories to everyday situations helped him improve his understanding. Ibrahim was always a talkative child and liked to be involved in adult conversations, but he still tended to interrupt and use inappropriate words.

He was now able to have a bath without my help. At times he spent a long time in the bath because he tended to get carried away playing imaginary games and talking to himself. Ibrahim always needed to play with toys in the bath and he still does this today. He loses track of time very easily, especially when he is enjoying himself. I can't remember exactly how old he was when I let him have his first shower without me being present. He still needed reminding to use body lotion after bathing, and I still had to tell him to clean his ears with cotton buds and comb his hair after washing. It took a long time for him to remember to do this without being reminded constantly, but it did pay off in the end. I felt he achieved a milestone when he started to become more independent, but he still needed guiding and prompting a lot of the time. I could tell him to do the same thing one day, but he would still need to be reminded to do it the following day. Ibrahim never used the mirror to look at himself; I was like his mirror. He never remembered to comb his hair and most of the time it looked untidy. It just did not occur to him that he should be doing this everyday and that everyone else did this. It was a daily routine he had to learn to get used to, but I was pleased that he was still making progress in little ways.

CHAPTER 9

OVERCOMING THE LANGUAGE BARRIERS

Jane Speake, a speech therapist, whom Ibrahim worked with at school, suggested that Dr Patrick Bolton, who was an Honorary Consultant in child and adolescent psychiatry, should see Ibrahim. We had an appointment in July 1999 and Dr Bolton's assessment was very thorough and helpful. We discussed Ibrahim's history from his birth through to the present day. Everything about him was talked about including his eating habits, violence, tantrums, lack of communication – we went through the lot. Ibrahim was made to do small tasks without me being present. Most children dislike having to do any type of tests but Ibrahim thoroughly enjoyed them. He has always liked assessments and any sort of tests. His report stated: 'The combination of social and communication impairments with unusual interest patterns is suggestive of pervasive developmental disorder (autism spectrum disorder)'. I think that this was the first time he was labelled. This diagnosis helped a great deal and afterwards I spent a lot of time searching for information, something I should have done a long time ago. I was now interested in anything that contained information on PDD. Everything was beginning to make sense, but whatever label was given to him, he was still Ibrahim my son.

Between 1997 and 1999 Ibrahim made great progress in response to the intensive help he had received at the speech and language centre. This was the most challenging period and the one when he made the most significant improvement. Ibrahim had made excellent progress and all the teachers and helpers who were involved with Ibrahim were working very hard. The teachers decided that as Ibrahim was doing so incredibly well; it was time to move on. After a statutory review meeting, it was decided that, with support, Ibrahim would integrate into Arbury mainstream school from September 1999. He had attended some lessons in the main school, mostly in the afternoon, for topic work and some language work in his last academic year. I felt extremely pleased with this decision, but I was also concerned about whether Ibrahim would be able to cope with this change.

Ibrahim was allocated only four hours LSA support per week, which did not seem much at all. Would he be able to work independently? I was worried and thought that Ibrahim would be heavily dependant on teacher support, as he was used to this at the speech and language centre. At this time, I was very concerned about the effect it would have on Ibrahim. Ibrahim was not used to working alone as he had always needed someone to steer him in the right direction. However, the more I thought about it, the more I thought that perhaps now was the time to change this. I felt the right decision had been made and it was time to move on. He had to start being independent at some stage. Ibrahim did not like change; it upset him and changed his moods, but I felt now was the right time.

Ibrahim was finding it easier to get along with other children and understanding the needs and feelings of others was becoming easier for him. Ibrahim always liked people to follow his lead. He had developed more appropriate language for social purposes and was now maturing nicely and this was noticeable in some of his actions. He was a hard worker and liked to please in whatever he did, but sometimes he tried too hard and would end up making silly and avoidable mistakes. He enjoyed being involved in adult conversations even when sometimes it was inappropriate. At times he could be too talkative and he would ramble on and on, interrupting my conversations with other people by making irrelevant comments. This was annoying and was definitely something that needed to be stopped.

Despite Ibrahim's difficulties, his behaviour was good most of the time. However, he had his moments, just like all children do. He was very protective of his younger brother Imran, and he took this responsibility to heart. He also had a habit of laughing and giggling inappropriately. His moods were awful, but bearable, but when he was in a foul mood he would mope around with a long face, sometimes for hours. It was at times like this when his brain would not work. It would shut down and he would get confused and tearful.

Ibrahim moved into mainstream school in September 1999. It wasn't as if he was moving to a new school, as he knew all the children in his class and they all knew him. I told Ibrahim not to forget to ask the teacher for help if he did not understand something. After all, that was what they were there for and Ibrahim needed to know that it was not shameful to ask for help. At times he would think that by forgetting a problem, it would just go away. This was the way he dealt with so many issues that he didn't want to face. I explained to him how to deal with difficulties even if he could not find the right answer to his problem and this helped build up his self-esteem. Ibrahim was quite a sensitive boy and he would get upset over trivial things, for example, seeing a baby cry would upset him. Most of the time, he tried to hide his tears. It was easy to see that he was upset but I would overlook this and pretend that I did not notice, otherwise it would make him even more embarrassed and he would be angry with me for gloating about it.

Ibrahim always listened attentively during class discussions. He was happy to make his own contribution but always spoke first and did his thinking later. Often he was unable to articulate the answer because he had misunderstood the question altogether. He was always encouraged to spend longer thinking about the question before rushing to put his hand up to give an answer. Ibrahim still had difficulties with comprehension. He was able to understand the literal interpretation, but found it harder to think about why characters behaved as they did or how they were feeling.

Despite all these difficulties and my own worries, Ibrahim's integration into mainstream school proved a success. He proved us all wrong. However, Ibrahim often felt the need to tell tales about things he saw going on in class. I think initially he found it difficult to cope with things going on around him, as it was busier than at the centre. He would often complain that someone had knocked him or that someone was not doing as they were told. Both his teacher and I had to teach him the things to ignore and the things that were important to pay attention to in class. I realised that Ibrahim telling tales would make him an unpopular member of the class and that it was something he had to learn not to do.

In the summer holidays, Ibrahim liked to play with other children who lived nearby. There were occasions when he would lose track of time and because he would carry on playing for hours, I would constantly check to see if he was safe. I would always tell him what time to come home for lunch or tea, only to have him forget as he was so absorbed in playing that he would forget everything else. This was something that was going to take a great deal of time to improve.

One day he went to a paddling pool, a few minutes away from our house with some friends. It was quite hot on that particular day. Ibrahim took his watch off and put it down on the grass. He played in the pool for about thirty minutes when he decided to return home. He went to the place where he had left his watch only to discover it was gone. Someone had obviously taken it. Ibrahim returned home very upset. At first, I thought that he had been attacked because of the state he was in. However, he seemed to know the boy who he thought had taken it, but he did not know where he lived. I had to explain to Ibrahim never to leave valuables and personal possessions in public places as people steal things. I felt guilty not explaining situations like this before it actually occurred. At times like this, Ibrahim would not know how to cope with the situation. He was not aware that anything could be taken from him if he was careless; Ibrahim was more vulnerable than other children his age. I told him not to worry and that I could always buy him another watch. He did not feel like playing with his friends for a few days after that. I should have realised that this could have happened to him at any time and it taught us both a lesson. Ibrahim had become a victim of a petty crime and it was hard for him to understand this situation because it made him feel useless and a failure. Ibrahim was vulnerable and something like this was bound to happen sometime, but I felt it was a pity it occurred in this way.

CHAPTER 10

GOTTA CATCH THEM ALL!

Do you remember the Pokemon card-collecting phase that all children went through? What a nightmare! I did not realise how much disruption it would cause in Ibrahim's life. It all started when I took Ibrahim on a visit to the Forbidden Planet where I bought him a Pokemon cards starter pack. Ibrahim really enjoyed watching the cartoons and hardly missed an episode at all. What a big mistake buying those cards was. Almost everyday after that, Ibrahim would constantly nag me to buy him some more cards. His uncle bought him some and so did his dad. We all thought it was relatively harmless, but every time we went shopping and saw Pokemon cards, he urged me to buy him some. I did not always give in to him, but if Ibrahim did not get his own way he would sulk miserably. He would walk off, completely ignoring me, and would have a long face for hours. This was part of his behavioural problems. I tried every way to reason with him but at times I relented and bought him some in order to get some peace.

Ibrahim was into Pokemon everything. I bought him reading books to divert his interest from the cards. He was given a Pokemon t-shirt, slippers, annuals, notebooks, etc. Ibrahim always received more presents than his other cousins from members of the family. He started to swap his duplicated cards at school, until his teachers decided to ban them as many children were quarrelling over them. He even bought Pokemon cards with money that he had been given to him as a present. It was a total waste of money and I tried to make him realise this. He did not know how to spend money wisely. Ibrahim had about one hundred cards enclosed in a smart wallet to keep them in good condition and he also had many swaps. Ibrahim was so protective of his cards.

Once he went shopping with his nana. Ibrahim asked his nana if he could buy some Pokemon cards, but she said no, as he had gone with her to keep her company and not for her to buy him things. He sulked throughout the entire trip, hiding in corners so that his nana had to go looking for him. He was seeking attention and I was very cross to discover that he had tried to manipulate his nana. I really did not know what to do and how to shift his interest elsewhere. This really tested my patience and I seemed to be getting cross with Ibrahim whenever he mentioned Pokemon cards. Over the years, Ibrahim's interest in Pokemon hasn't faded. He still loves them just as much as he did at the start, but thankfully he is not as obsessed with them now as he was then. It was very difficult to satisfy his interests.

Ibrahim soon moved on to another obsession, this time it was with the television programme, *Who Wants to be a Millionaire?* In the first two or three series of the programme, he did not miss one episode. At times the programme clashed with another programme we wanted to see, and Ibrahim would go into one of his tremendous sulks when we decided to watch something else. It was usually on four times a week and I explained that he had the chance to watch it later in the week, so it did not matter if he missed an episode. He did not understand this and it proved so difficult to reason with him. This infatuation with the programme drove me so mad that I eventually resented it and I could not bear to watch the programme. He would talk about it all the time and after watching the programme he would play the game, making up questions and writing them down and pretending to be Chris Tarrant. He was truly obsessed with it. We decided to buy him the board game for his birthday that year. I thought it would do him no harm and perhaps help him get over his obsession in time. He learnt a great deal from the general knowledge questions, so I suppose this obsession had its good points.

Ibrahim showed a special interest in reference books and encyclopaedias. He was still inquisitive about numbers and was now interested in weather forecasts and liked to talk about the weather. He would spend a lot of time learning the information and he insisted on checking the teletext weather forecast everyday. Sport was another interest, but instead of watching the actual game, Ibrahim preferred to look at the results on the teletext and then write them down in his notebook in his best handwriting. He did this everyday and it turned into another obsession. He wasted a lot of time, because he was more interested in watching the results change on the teletext than watching the game itself. I would look at him meticulously taking notes and wondered what pleasure he derived from such an activity. I tried to encourage him to watch the actual sport so that the results would make more sense, but he wasn't interested and simply carried on viewing the results. This was another aspect to the complex nature and behaviour that was Ibrahim.

CHAPTER 11

I CAN'T EAT IT!
I WON'T EAT IT!

I have already mentioned Ibrahim's problems with food. Ibrahim has always been awkward where eating is concerned, and he has never been willing to try new foods, despite lots of encouragement. With the foods he does not like, he refuses even to touch the packaging that they are contained in, as if the packaging was contaminated and he would catch something if he touched it. There was one occasion when I told him to give Imran a packet of crisps. He was not happy about touching the packet so he pinched the edge of it, not holding the whole packet in his hand as he handed it to Imran. It was as though he was touching something absolutely disgusting. Ibrahim disliked any type of sauce and he has never eaten any flavour of yoghurt, fromage frais or crisps. He would not eat breakfast cereals either and his choice of chocolates was limited too. Ibrahim only ate plain chocolate. He wouldn't eat any caramel or wafer-type chocolates or anything that contained nuts. Once again, this highlighted how different he was from most children who are happy to try new varieties of chocolate.

Ibrahim eventually started to eat burgers, but he would only have cheeseburgers containing lettuce only and nothing else. He did not eat chips, although most children love chips. He refused to look at the foods he did not like, which he still does now. There were phases he would go through for days and weeks on end. For a while he had a fixation on Del Monte pure orange juice and he used to drink two to three glasses a day. He would not drink juice of any other brand and at times it was as though he would drink too much, but suddenly he would completely change and not touch a drop. He is now into Apple Juice and will not drink any other type of juice, and of course, it had to be Del Monte.

Another phase he went through was at breakfast, when he would only eat two Bird's Eye potato waffles, two fried eggs, with the egg white thrown away and fried mushrooms. He had this for breakfast everyday for weeks, until he got bored and then he moved onto scrambled eggs on toast. Ibrahim would only eat Hovis medium sliced bread and no other brand.

Once, Ibrahim stayed for the night at his uncle's house. At breakfast, he made a point of checking the type of bread his uncle had. It had to be Hovis white bread and no other brand otherwise he would not eat it. He would rather stay hungry than try a new brand. He can still be very fussy about food and this can be very frustrating at times. I became so annoyed about this constant fussiness with food, but I shouldn't have been surprised because it was typical of Ibrahim.

Ibrahim liked Cadbury's drinking chocolate. We would usually shop at Budgens, so I would buy their own brand of milk. We moved house in October 2001 and now started shopping at Sainsbury's, which was more convenient. I noticed one day he was not drinking any milk, as there seemed to be more milk in the fridge than usual. Ibrahim made his own drink by heating milk in a mug in the microwave, then adding drinking chocolate and some sugar. It had to be Cadbury's. I asked him why he wasn't drinking milk any more, and he replied, 'I only like Budgens milk and I don't like Sainsbury milk.' I couldn't understand the difference between the two milks. After much talk and explaining that most milk comes from the same dairies, he started to drink Sainsbury's milk, but at times I thought he was only drinking it to placate me. Now he is reluctant to drink any brand of milk unless it is gold top, which I bought for cooking purposes and he decided to try it. At least he is having some milk, so I should not complain.

We had the same problems with fresh cream. He only liked Co-op single cream, no other brand with his Coco Pops. Ibrahim would only eat Coco Pops with cream or he wouldn't eat them at all, and the Coco Pops had to be Kellogg's. I had to make special trips to the Co-op just to buy their own brand of single cream. Once, I decided to be crafty and bought Budgens single cream instead and poured it into a Co-op single cream carton, which I had kept from the last occasion he had it. It worked. He did not notice a difference at all. So I decided to do this again when Ibrahim finished another carton. However, on the third occasion, Ibrahim realised that something was not quite right. He told me that the cream was thinner than usual, which it was, and tasted slightly different. Ibrahim knew that it was not his usual cream. He realised what I had done and was fooled no more. He was reluctant to have any more cream after that, although I had started to buy him the Co-op brand again. It took a lot of convincing that it was his normal cream and I ended up having to prove it by showing him the shopping receipts. Children who have specific dietary problems cannot be fooled in this way because they are more aware of tastes than we realise. Ibrahim and I had learnt something new.

Ibrahim will sometimes eat apples, conference pears and raisins, but he is unwilling to try other fruits. He once tried a piece of banana, after much persuasion, but ended up feeling very sick. This taught me not to be too persistent in getting him to try new foods. It was as though his brain had already decided if he would like a particular food before he had given himself a chance to try it first. The food talked to Ibrahim. It would say, 'Don't eat me; I am not good for you!' It was always the food versus Ibrahim and Ibrahim was always the winner of this war, although I think he thought it was mum versus Ibrahim when it came to food. When he became ill, Ibrahim refused to take anything to reduce his temperature such as foul-tasting medicine. I mixed some Calpol in his Ribena drink to disguise it, but he always knew what I had done. He always seemed to be one step ahead of me and there was no fooling him. It wasn't until he reached the age of eight when, after much persuasion, he took his first spoon of medicine.

Although Ibrahim's diet was improving very gradually, I felt he was not getting the right nutrients, so I decided that he should take chocolate-flavoured Build-up. This was a vitamin-enriched supplement in powder form to be mixed with milk. Ibrahim was willing to drink this as long as it was chocolate flavour. For a few days he drank this three times a day after his meals, as a top up, but we discovered that it upset his stomach so he had to stop drinking it. He was not willing to take any other sort of vitamin supplements until the age of about ten, when he was prepared to take Haliborange vitamin syrup. This contained real orange juice, which he did not seem to mind, but after a few weeks he decided that he developed a dislike for it and would not take it anymore.

Ibrahim was continuing to experience difficulties with communication and there was a discrepancy between his general level of ability and his language skills. It was thought that his general level of ability was within the average range or even slightly above, but his language scores were well below average. Ibrahim was assessed annually for his Statutory Review Report.

Ibrahim's ability to listen to and follow specific instructions was good at times. However, he found it difficult to infer meaning and his ability to understand information also reflected in his knowledge of what words meant. Furthermore, his ability to carry out instructions successfully was also dependent on his ability to remain focused when instructions were presented to him.

Ibrahim was able to remember fairly complex vocabulary that he heard and he always enjoyed attempting to spell these words. However, his understanding of their definition was poor and this often led to confusion. Ibrahim had a tendency to develop a very simple or narrow definition of a word and needed help to expand this. He was able to explain what was happening in a picture, but Ibrahim found it difficult to interpret information presented in this way. Therefore, he was able to construct a sentence about what he was able to see before him, but when he was asked to think beyond this, he became confused.

Ibrahim found it difficult to explain why someone may be feeling a particular way and found it difficult to imagine himself in a similar situation and consider possible solutions. His understanding of the vocabulary used also affected his success. For example, Ibrahim confused witness with victim and he thought supervision was linked with eyesight. One can see why. Ibrahim could recall simple clear sentences accurately but his attention span was variable and he would sometimes switch off completely and he was unable to attempt simple pieces of work. Being under pressure confused him and he became mixed up when he tried too hard. Ibrahim was always determined to try and remember all that he had heard, but occasionally his auditory memory was overstretched. He was able to produce rather long sentences with lots of information, but it was difficult for him to be salient – he always wanted to add more. Sometimes this was useful in a discussion, but he seemed to find it hard to control himself or to know when it was appropriate to give more information and when to stop.

By this time, Ibrahim had developed some very appropriate friendships, engaging in cheerful and meaningful conversations with other people. This meant his social skills were improving, but he still had difficulties with personal organisation, at home and at school. At school it would be forgetting to bring homework or letters home, or he would forget to pass on a simple message. This was an area in which he needed a lot of prompting and reminding. To aid this, I began to write small notes and placed them in his bag for him to remember, which he did not like at all. This was because other children did not need notes in their bags and he would say to me, 'I will start to remember now. I won't forget!' Sadly, this was something that caused me to shout at him, because I thought that after reminding him about the same thing day after day, he would remember by now. This was not the case at all and it became a big problem. For some people, this may seem to be a small problem, but for me, these small things mattered. It was an important skill which he had to learn himself.

One time, when Ibrahim was in year 5, he forgot to bring a letter home regarding a school residential trip which involved making an advanced booking. He had forgotten all about it until a teacher sent a letter home confirming that the trip was booked. It was then too

73

late to allow Ibrahim to be able to go on the trip. I was very disappointed by this, as most of his classmates were going. Ibrahim was concerned that he would be made fun of because it looked as though we were unable to afford to pay for the trip. I explained that if he had given me the letter in time, he could have gone. I was trying to instil in him the importance of remembering things and being reliable.

Ibrahim was still experiencing difficulties when he was supposed to be sitting still on the carpet with his class. He spent a lot of time fiddling with his fingers and his shoes. Ibrahim had to be admonished by his teacher frequently and would pay attention for a while, but would then start fiddling about again. This became a common occurrence and it was necessary to have an adult sitting by him to prompt him to focus his attention.

Ibrahim was able to retain a large number of facts and pieces of information. His distractibility and high-level language difficulties made it hard for him to sort out which information was relevant to the task he had to perform. He was working on a topic about space and was given a booklet about the moon and told to write three pieces of relevant information from the book. Ibrahim was unable to do this succinctly. Unaided, he wrote the following three facts:

1. The first person to walk on the moon was Neil Armstrong (this was suggested by others in the class).
2. The closest distance 221,467 miles.
3. 51 to earth's orbit.

Ibrahim had been unable to think of three different headings under which to classify the information he had found, which had been the first requirement of the task. He needed help with this from his teacher. He then needed one to one assistance to extract further information from the textbooks. His good memory can give a false impression of his level of comprehension. An example of this is some work he did on adverbs. He was unable to describe what an adverb was, but was able to name some adverbs. He came up with, 'nippingly' and 'wealthily'. This showed a lack of real understanding.

Ibrahim was asked to say how pairs of words were different. With this task, he was able to give some very good answers but with others he missed out vital information. This reflected his difficulty with saliency and with organising his knowledge. The following two tasks are from the six-year-old level.

> *A man–A dog.* Ibrahim said, 'A dog is an animal, a man is a
> human being.'
> *Wood-glass.* Ibrahim said, 'Glass can break; wood you need
> a saw to cut through. Glass is no kind of colour, wood is
> brownish.'
> A question was asked, 'Why do we use glass in windows?'
> Ibrahim replied, 'You can open the glass.'
> He was asked, 'Why don't we use wood for windows?'
> He replied, 'Wood is opaque and glass is transparent.'

This clearly illustrates Ibrahim's difficulty with applying his knowledge. Ibrahim was also assessed on his inferential reading comprehension where his performance proved inconsistent. He was able to give some very good answers, but also showed areas where he had not understood. It was necessary for him to study each text for some time before giving answers. This showed that on his first reading he was unable to absorb information. Ibrahim was asked if a creature in the text he read had feet. Ibrahim said, 'Yes', which was the correct answer, but when he was asked how he knew, he replied, 'I was just guessing.' He had missed the information, which referred to the creatures muddy footprints. Another was about a family replacing an old garage because they needed a larger one for their new car. Ibrahim was asked, 'Do they live in a new house?' He replied, 'Yes, because they are going to get a new car.' This clearly demonstrated that he found difficulties in areas of inferential comprehension, knowing which information is important, organizing the information and application of knowledge.

Ibrahim's difficulties have made it hard for me to fully understand him the way that I should, despite being the closest person to him. It was always easy to forget that he had problems in almost all aspects of his life. It has affected everything about him, his diet, understanding, social skills and language, so how can one expect him to lead a normal life? It put an enormous strain on all our lives and it was easy to compare him with other children. It was as though I was trying to fight two battles, the first to understand Ibrahim and the difficulties he was diagnosed with, and second, to convince the other people in my family of his problems. I always felt lost and a failure and inevitably I blamed myself for this situation.

Every time Ibrahim progressed, I felt very proud and forgot all the stresses I had experienced, although it would take just one tactless comment from someone and I would feel like a failure again. I was on a rollercoaster. – everyday it was a high or low situation. I would sit and cry about it sometimes when I lay down to sleep. I would look at Ibrahim when he slept at night, thinking he looked so innocent, as though there was nothing wrong with him. This was my thinking time when I reflected on the day's events. It was a difficult time for me, although I never showed my tension to anyone and I taught myself to conceal my feelings. I did not want sympathy because that would not change anything. Dealing with Ibrahim also taught me to be strong – I had to be for my son's sake. I realised that getting into a state would not help him at all. I feel I have prematurely aged and, although I am now thirty-one, I feel about forty.

I was more relaxed with Imran. He was perfectly normal and I had no worries about him. His speech developed properly at the age of three and a half, before he went to nursery school. His diet was average, his social skills were evident and he related to other children well. For me it felt amazing, as I had not gone through this with Ibrahim. It was difficult to believe that Ibrahim and Imran were brothers. They were very different indeed.

CHAPTER 12

NEW CHALLENGES EVERY DAY

In July 2000, Ibrahim's second brother Aniq was born. Ibrahim and Imran came to visit me in hospital on the day he was born. Ibrahim was missing me more than Imran was. He told me to come home as soon as possible and became very emotional. He was taken care of by his nana and his father until I returned home the following day. Ibrahim was now ten years old and seemed proud of being the eldest of his three brothers and he started to become much more mature.

Ibrahim still found it difficult taking messages or recalling what someone may have said to him, and this seemed to be an everyday occurrence. On occasions, it was necessary for Ibrahim to answer the phone and take a message if I was occupied with something else at that time. I would ask Ibrahim who had called and he would be able to tell me without hesitation, but when I asked what the person had said, he was unable to recall this accurately. He became confused, not knowing what to tell me first. So I always had to run through a series of questions to be able to find out what the caller had said, even if the conversation had only been 5 minutes ago. After many times, I thought it would be better for Ibrahim to make notes during a phone call and I went through what were the most important things to write down. When Ibrahim became very confused, he would start to become upset and would end up sulking for the rest of the day. Other people found this hard to understand. They could not make out why Ibrahim was able to forget a short simple conversation that occurred only a few moments earlier. Having said this, I would often ask myself the same question.

At this age I felt that Ibrahim was able to go to the shop by himself, which was only five minutes away. Usually, I sent him to do simple things, such as post a letter which already had a stamp on it, or to buy a small item from the shop. Once, I sent him to buy a pre-packed bunch of bananas. He knew which ones they were, as we had bought them many times before. However, Ibrahim came home with a bunch of bruised, half squashed, half-rotten bananas, black in colour. I did not even think to tell him to check the bananas for freshness or to see whether they were bruised or not. I did not get cross, as I felt it was my fault for not explaining this to him beforehand. This taught me to not to assume that Ibrahim would know and understand everything. It may come naturally to others, but not to him.

I would watch Ibrahim from the door as he was returning home. Most of the time, he would talk to himself, as though he was not completely alert to everything that was around him. I always told him the dangers about talking to strangers and he had a good concept of this. Ibrahim had a habit of talking to himself in inappropriate places, for example, in the shower, toilet or when watching television, when he would talk about whether he liked a particular programme. He would talk as though someone was with him. I have been told that many children with the same difficulties as Ibrahim talk to themselves. I told him not to do this when he was outside, because people may find it strange. He still does this even today and has been doing this since he was very young and I think it gives him a sense of security.

Ibrahim did not understand sarcasm at all. Most of our family members liked to be sarcastic and joke around with him, but he did not find jokes very amusing and would get upset by them. It took a long time before Ibrahim started to understand jokes, but I suppose most children find jokes difficult to understand. He was now receiving fewer speech therapy sessions, but it was decided he would benefit from further social skill sessions. Ibrahim attended six sessions in the summer holiday of 2000. The sessions were very beneficial and he demonstrated that he was very familiar with the rules of listening, thinking, looking and taking turns. He still required support to concentrate on a particular task, and he found it difficult to sustain his attention in a distracting environment. I explained to Ibrahim that he should try to apply the knowledge he learnt at the social skills group in everyday situations.

Ibrahim's knowledge of the Bengali language was improving a great deal, but he still found it difficult to explain things properly. It was because his knowledge of the Bengali vocabulary was limited and we tried to practise everyday. He had always found Bengali difficult and still does. When Ibrahim talks, he speaks with an English accent and it has always been difficult for him having a speech difficulty and trying to learn two languages simultaneously. At times, close family would comment that he could not speak Bengali as well as he should because we speak too much English.

CHAPTER 13

'I JUST WANT TO BE ABLE TO TALK PROPERLY!'

Ibrahim continued to have difficulties in some situations involving inference and cause–effect, where the situations were outside his own experience. For instance, Ibrahim had to describe a picture, which showed an image of a bird's nest on the ground. He found it hard to give a good reason as to how this may have occurred. He thought that perhaps a larger bird might have moved it there. We had to talk about this and it took a lot of reasoning before Ibrahim could make sense of it. I still find this amusing and I remember when his teacher told me about this we couldn't stop laughing. Ibrahim could not always explain why something was a problem, for example, not having soap in the bath. He thought that soap was used to make your skin soft and he needed some discussion to discover that it helps one to get clean and kill germs. I think that he picked this up from the television adverts about soaps that make your skin soft.

His language difficulties reflected in some of his writing. Once, his teacher discussed with him a story about a meeting. Ibrahim had all the elements of the story written out, but was unable to connect two events within the story, which were one character getting up too late to go to the meeting, and the meeting having to be moved to a later time.

As explained previously, Ibrahim has had difficulties with his gross and fine motor skills. He would bump into things quite a lot and things still slipped out of his hand. When walking in the street together, he would not give the person he was walking with enough space to walk without bumping into them, which was usually me. If walking behind someone, he would virtually walk on top of them and we had to practise how to walk by giving people space on each side without bumping into them. It took a very long time to get this right. He found it difficult to walk in a straight line, as Ibrahim had trouble with his legs. Although he was able to walk, there was something not quite right, as though his right leg constantly bumped into his left leg causing him to trip over. Ibrahim's legs were not as strong as they should be. I had to teach him to allow space between his legs and walk in a straight line, but he would concentrate so hard on doing this that he would forget to look ahead of him causing him to bump into something.

When Ibrahim was about four years old, he rode a bicycle with stabilizers, but he would constantly fall off. Today, after much perseverance, Ibrahim can ride a bike. I didn't fully understand that Ibrahim had difficulties with his legs at the beginning, although I found it hard to understand how he could keep tripping himself up. Ibrahim had noticeably long arms with long, slender fingers. Manual tasks were the most difficult for him. At times, I could see the frustration in his face. It would break my heart because he would say, 'I wish there was nothing wrong with me and I wish I was normal.' I really felt for him when he said such things, and longed for all his problems to disappear.

I talked with one of Ibrahim's specialist teachers about my concerns with his motor skills. I think this should have been looked at earlier, but for some reason it was overlooked and his difficulties with expressive language had been given much more attention. I was asked to fill in a form so that specialists could assess Ibrahim further. In June 2001, an appointment was made for Ibrahim to be seen by an occupational therapist and a physiotherapist. He tried very hard in all activities, but at times he seemed as if he was struggling. The clinical observations were that Ibrahim had poor joint stability especially in his hands and arms. For activities requiring balance, Ibrahim relied heavily on visual clues. He had difficulty in moving his head independently of his body and also struggled with activities requiring accurate proprioception (body position awareness).

Ibrahim had difficulties co-ordinating fine movements of his hands quickly and often fumbled. When grasping small objects such as pegs, he demonstrated irregular grasp patterns. The way he gripped a pencil was abnormal too, holding it between his thumb and all of his fingers, wrist in flexion and his forearm in mid position. Despite this, he has beautiful writing. Watching him write with his unusual pencil grip, it is hard to believe his handwriting is so very neat and tidy. The tip of his thumb is very hyperextended. I remember that my sister's thumb was exactly the same and maybe this runs in the family. He lacked stability and proprioception in his hands and he has low muscle tone and poor joint stability. I feel that this will be a long term condition and possibly will be with him for all his life. When looking at him, one can see that he looks weak and vulnerable. His looks explain all and people judge him on his appearance, which is very sad. Ibrahim has many good qualities and it is unfair to judge him by his looks, but I suppose it is natural for someone to do this.

There are many minor things that Ibrahim finds difficult. For example, it took him a long time to learn how to tie his shoelaces. I had to tie them for him everyday. He also found it tricky to spread butter on bread or hold a knife and fork in the traditional manner. The small things we take for granted are the things that Ibrahim finds difficult. Ibrahim has learnt to cope in his own way and he knew this was a battle he had to fight. I had to talk to him about his difficulties, but it was as if I was talking to him about something that he did not fully understand. I helped him to realise that sometimes he would be frustrated with not being able to express language in the way in which he wanted to. I also explained that there were practical things that he would take time to master, such as his shoelaces. All the time, I made sure he understood that I had confidence in him and I knew he would get there in the end.

In July 2001 Ibrahim went on a trip to London with his Islamic school. They went to the Regents Park Mosque and then on to the Natural History Museum. The teachers at the school had never been fully aware of Ibrahim's difficulties. He had always done very well and was advanced in his Arabic learning. Ibrahim and I prepared his lunch together. I told him what to have for lunch and what to have for afternoon snack time. He seemed very confident and understood everything. I allowed Ibrahim to take a camera to take pictures as I thought he was would be able to manage this. I felt sure the trip would go very well and Ibrahim was very excited.

Ibrahim returned home with half of his lunch uneaten. He had been carrying his heavy rucksack throughout the journey and could have made it lighter if he had eaten most of his lunch. In the front pocket of his rucksack I had put a piece of quiche in a small container and a galaxy chocolate drink. I took it out of his bag and Ibrahim said, 'Whoops, I forgot I had that.' We talked about the trip and I realised that it had not occurred to him to check his bag. During the trip, Ibrahim went on a picnic in the park with the rest of the class, but instead of eating his lunch, he got carried away playing with the other boys. He had to have a quick lunch in the coach on the way to the museum in the afternoon. Nobody had told him it was time to have lunch. They probably assumed that as they were all going to the park to have lunch that they all knew, as it had been discussed beforehand. What they did not realise was that Ibrahim needed to be told again, because of his difficulties in understanding the obvious.

I was very cross, because we had talked about everything and I was confident that he would not have any problems and that he had understood. However, once again I was proved wrong. This was part of Ibrahim's problem and I realised that I should have written everything down on paper for him and shouldn't have relied on his memory. I told myself that I would do this next time we came across a similar situation. I took a step too far ahead, so it was time to take a step back and remember this next time. It was not his fault, but it was something that he would need a lot of help with in the future.

Ibrahim was becoming more confident in doing things. He was a confident speaker and this was especially noticeable in class. He was becoming more organized and was an excellent reader, demonstrating this through expression and fluency. Ibrahim particularly enjoyed reading non-fiction. He always read out loud at home, as if he was reading to an audience. His spelling was at an adult level. Ibrahim had spelling tests every week at school from the beginning of year six and he never misspelled a word. Ibrahim was well known for this and he is even a better speller than me.

Ibrahim was at last able to write imaginative stories. He had a good awareness of the reader and audience and was able to vary his writing accordingly. His use of punctuation was excellent and he was able to use advanced vocabulary and sentence structure in story writing, which was good. It was easy to forget that he had had difficulties in the past, as he was doing extremely well in this. He spent time at home writing stories, but at times could get carried away. His stories were either about space or Pokemon adventures. I would find bits of paper that had half written stories on them scattered all over the house. He would not complete his stories, but would lose interest and move onto the next one using a fresh piece of paper.

We decided to allow Ibrahim to go on a residential school trip to Graffam Water Centre, near Huntingdon for two nights. I felt confident he would cope well. I really missed him, but felt sure that he was enjoying himself. That is, until he decided to phone me on the night before he was due back. Ibrahim seemed upset and told me he missed me and that something awful had happened. He said his towel had been stolen. He could not find it after his shower and did not tell the teacher. I told Ibrahim to get his teacher to talk to me on the phone and I explained to her what Ibrahim had told me. She said that his towel was probably lost and not stolen and wondered why Ibrahim did not tell her. She also said that usually they don't allow children to phone home but that Ibrahim had persisted because he was missing home very much. When Ibrahim returned home, he told me that someone had entered the Centre and stolen medicine, money and a credit card belonging to the staff and that is why he thought that his towel had been stolen, because he could not find it. Typically, he immediately jumped to this conclusion before thinking about any other reasons.

This was not Ibrahim's first residential school trip. He had stayed at The Jarman Centre in Newmarket in July 1999, with teachers and children from his speech and language centre. He had eaten Linda McCartney's pies for every meal except breakfast. I had to give his teachers a list of all the foods he liked to eat, but at the Water Centre, Ibrahim was able to eat most foods and coped well. The trip taught him to appreciate home and myself much more. He really did miss me and I think it did him good being away from home.

Ibrahim did very well in his Key Stage 2 SATS tests and I was very proud of him. He had worked very hard during year six. A few years ago, I would never have imagined that he would be able to do so well in his schoolwork. The staff at Arbury School had worked extremely hard over the years to help him and I will never forget this. Towards the end of year six, in July 2002, Ibrahim was starting to feel the emotion of having to leave Arbury School and move onto secondary school. He would be the only child to go to the Netherhall School from Arbury, but once again it was time for Ibrahim to move on. It was time for a change. I think that this was the most worrying time for me and I'm sure I was worried more than Ibrahim was.

During the last two weeks of term, the children of year five and six were involved in a production of *Oliver*. Ibrahim played the part of Dr Grimwig. He was pleased that he had a speaking part. He had thirteen lines to learn and we practised every night at home, but he had no problem remembering them. Ibrahim's uncle and I went to see the first showing of the production. Ibrahim appeared in act two. I was so proud of him, as he looked very smart and spoke his lines loud and clear. I nearly cried at the end. After the play he told me he did not feel nervous at all but that he tried to imagine that no one was there. Obviously, nerves did not bother Ibrahim.

Ibrahim's school organised a leavers' party for all the year six pupils and it was an extremely emotional time. Ibrahim took part in a small play called *Billy Goats Gruffs' Grandchildren* which was about moving on. Ibrahim was presented with a pocket dictionary, as were the other children. Jane Rickell, the headmistress of the school, said to Ibrahim, 'I'll look out for you and I know you'll be very successful Ibrahim.' At that time, Ibrahim nearly cried. He was very emotional right until the last minute of school. He told me that he would probably never see his whole class together ever again, which was a sad thought. My mind wandered back to the day he first started at Arbury and now the last day had come. Ibrahim had been incapable of socialising with the children in the correct manner on his first day, and yet here he was with so many friends. He had been through many changes and I didn't imagine I would ever see this day. At the peak of his difficulties, it seemed as if our problems were never ending and things would never improve. I had been stressed, heartbroken and depressed and had felt like an old woman; now I felt overwhelmed.

Ibrahim still has difficulties with expressive language. He is not currently receiving any therapy or any other type of help. He still experiences difficulties with his fine and gross motor skills and this will probably be so for the rest of his life. Ibrahim is learning karate as I hope this may make a slight difference in helping him to become stronger. It does not matter to me what people think of him or his difficulties. I see Ibrahim as a normal boy. It is not his fault that he has learning difficulties, nor is it my fault. It has taught us both valuable lessons in life and his dad has learnt much about his difficulties too. We have all had the benefit of learning from different experiences which have helped us grow in various ways.

CHAPTER 14

FROM PRIMARY TO SECONDARY— IBRAHIM'S GREATEST TEST OF ALL

Ibrahim started secondary school in September 2002. This was an anxious time for me. I was concerned that he would have difficulties organising himself at school. He had to know what to put in his locker, how to look after his lunch money and locker key, and not leave his coat and PE kit behind when he moved classrooms. He had to make sure that he had all of his stationery equipment after every lesson as well as his books. It was something he had to do himself although I talked about this all the time so he would remember at school. There was a lot to remember and at times he would become visibly stressed by it, saying that there was too much to take in. I allowed time for him to get used to things, but he needed a lot of prompting and reminding as it was such a big change for him to deal with. It seemed at times that I was more worried than he was and Ibrahim could not understand what all the fuss was about. He had to realise that he needed to become much more independent than he had been before, and I would not always be around to sort out his problems for him.

One important thing that Ibrahim had to learn to do everyday was to look at himself in the mirror to check his appearance before going to school. This may seem amazing to other people, but it did not occur to Ibrahim to do this and it was not something he was used to doing. He was not very good at remembering to brush his hair or wipe clean his glasses, and he still needs reminding to brush his hair after he has washed it. I need to tell him to lay his towel out to dry but he still leaves it on the bathroom floor – typical boy! I still find his pyjamas lying on the floor after he has gone to school, but I expect most young people his age still do this. I sometimes wonder when he will remember to do these things without me having to remind him all the time. For now, Ibrahim has become used to the everyday routine of his new school and he has accepted that life is much busier than it was before. He does his homework at regular times without having to be reminded and he is better able to plan his time.

Ibrahim is still strict with his diet. He still only drinks Gold Top milk and he will not touch any type of yogurt or dessert. He hardly eats any fruit and the only salad vegetable he is willing to eat is lettuce. He refuses to try tomatoes and cucumbers but overall his diet is good compared to how it used to be. It would be great if he would include more variety in his diet as it would save me time as I often have to cook something separate for him. However, he is now eating most of the food we eat as a family and maybe one day he will reach the stage when he will eat almost anything. It is very difficult not get impatient but I know that, in his own time, he will get there.

Ibrahim will eat almost anywhere now, even at other people's houses, but can become rather upset if someone is very persistent that he should eat something because they do not understand that he does not like it. To be polite, he will not say anything. He still experiences difficulties with his fine and gross motor skills; he struggles to hold a fork in the correct manner and has just mastered the skill of riding a bike. His unusual pen hold will never change. If he tries to correct it, it will only have a detrimental effect on his handwriting. These difficulties will stay with him for life, which to me as his mother is heartbreaking, but I know that Ibrahim is strong and can cope.

Ibrahim still needs to be guided in most things he does. However, he is able to cope with school without much help.

Expressive language is still an area of difficulty, but he is improving every day. Ibrahim is an intelligent boy and his difficulties can prevent him from progressing as quickly as he could. He is still vulnerable which can be a worry to me. His learning disorder will remain with him for the rest of his life and it is sad that it can sometimes be mistaken for his character. I hope that people in future will judge Ibrahim by his character and not his disorder because I know he is a sensible and bright boy.

I had to work very hard to make my own family understand about Ibrahim's learning disorder and to explain it can happen to anyone. I do feel I could have done more to help Ibrahim in the early stages of diagnosis, if only I had known then what I know now. However, I believe that more and more Bangladeshi children will have this disorder and hopefully it will be recognised and accepted in the future. We have been fortunate to receive much help from the various agencies in this country. If Ibrahim had lived in Bangladesh, then this type of help would not have been available. His behavioural difficulties would have been blamed on Ibrahim being possessed by evil spirits and people would have said that this was the work of the devil because sadly, in our community, this conclusion is not uncommon. I will be forever grateful for all the people who have given Ibrahim help and support over the years. Without their help, Ibrahim would not be where he is today.

To demonstrate how much Ibrahim's has improved, I'd like to include a poem he wrote which was selected along with other poems written by children of his age, and these poems were published in a book called 'The Write Stuff'.

The Midnight Run

I ran and ran as fast as I could
Not knowing what would happen and what should
It was easy to know I was in danger
Because I was being followed by a stranger.

My only friend was the moon
Maybe I'd be rescued soon
The hooded stranger was holding a knife
If he got near me, I would probably lose my life.

I ran to the end of a cliff
My arms and my legs were stiff
The man looked at me and waited
I knew for sure it was me he hated.

I turned round and looked down
A raging waterfall, very sure I had to drown
The man sniggered and looked at me
But then I jumped down and suddenly ...

I clung to a branch and looked relieved
This is probably a story you wouldn't believe
The branch snapped and I let out a piercing scream.
Huh? Wait a minute. It was only a dream!

I end this story by saying to parents with children who have similar difficulties, 'Never say never!' Children can progress in ways you never expect them too. I am grateful every day for the progress Ibrahim has made. And despite all the difficulties, I wouldn't change him for the world.

THE END

Printed in the United Kingdom
by Lightning Source UK Ltd.
135896UK00001B/4/A